Here is a clear, t s
– or anyone who of
experience and th t
resource for anyon

NAT SCHLUTER
Principal, Johannesburg Bible College, Johannesburg, South Africa

Eloff's careful and nuanced work in the text of James makes this an invaluable volume for anyone seeking to preach or teach from this rich letter. Especially useful are the section on the melodic line of the letter and clarity of the theme statements throughout. This is probably the best thing I've read on James.

ROBERT KINNEY
Director of Ministries, Simeon Trust

Mervyn Eloff has added another gem to an already treasured series. This absorbing volume comes from a preacher who has years of experience at both church pulpit and college lectern, a combination which has helped to produce a most accessible and beneficial guide to James' letter. Each chapter is generously filled with helpful insights and practical preaching points, all with plenty of incentives to get you looking deeper into the meaning of the text. One must also give particular mention to Mervyn's excellent work on finding that reportedly elusive theme of James. The focus on discovering the 'melodic-line' is one of the great strengths of this entire series and is an indispensable step for every diligent Bible teacher.

Reading through *Teaching James* has proved to be both challenging and encouraging. I've been convicted to address the all too familiar inconsistencies in my own life as well as stirred to convey these deeply applicable truths of James to others. May God use this book to give that same momentum to your Christian life and teaching.

GLENN LYONS
Presiding Bishop of REACH-South Africa

TEACHING
JAMES

From text to message

MERVYN ELOFF

SERIES EDITORS: JONATHAN GEMMELL & DAVID JACKMAN

PT RESOURCES

CHRISTIAN
FOCUS

Copyright © Proclamation Trust Media 2021

Paperback ISBN: 978-1-5271-0534-8
Ebook ISBN: 978-1-5271-0779-3

10 9 8 7 6 5 4 3 2 1

Published in 2021
by
Christian Focus Publications Ltd.,
Geanies House, Fearn, Ross-shire,
IV20 1TW, Scotland, Great Britain
www.christianfocus.com
with
Proclamation Trust Resources,
Willcox House, 140-148 Borough High Street,
London, SE1 1LB, England, Great Britain.
www.proctrust.org.uk

Cover design by Moose77.com

Printed and bound by
Bell & Bain, Glasgow

Contents

Author's Preface...7

Series Preface 9

How to Use This Book.. 11

Part One: Introducing James 15

   1. Getting Our Bearings in James 17

   2. Why Should We Preach and
      Teach James? 33

   3. Ideas for a Preaching or Teaching Series
      in James...37

Part Two: Teaching James...................................... 43

   1. A Significant Greeting (James 1:1)...........45

   2. The Path to Life (James 1:2-12)...............55

   3. Facing Temptation (James 1:13-18)..........71

   4. The Word-Shaped Life
      (James 1:19-25) 83

   5. True Religion (James 1:26-27) 93

   6. Seeing People God's Way
      (James 2:1-13) 103

   7. Faith That Saves (James 2:14-26)........... 115

   8. Words! Words! Words! (James 3:1-12) ... 129

   9. Wisdom for Life (James 3:13-18) 143

  10. Wholehearted Christianity
       (James 4:1-10) 155

  11. Whose World Is It Anyway?
       (James 4:11-12) 169

  12. God Willing! (James 4:13-17) 179

13. Exposed! (James 5:1-6) 189

14. Hopeful Perseverance (James 5:7-12) 199

15. A Call to Spiritual Restoration
    (James 5:13-20) 211

Further Reading 225

Author's Preface

As I write, South Africa, like many countries in the world, is in lockdown in an attempt to stem the spread of Covid-19. Activities that we took for granted, such as gathering at church on the Lord's Day, are no longer possible. And how we feel their loss! Indeed, there are times when it is hard to believe that anything will be 'normal' again.

How good it has been, in this time of trial, to return to James' remarkable letter. How encouraging to be reminded that God, the giver of every good and perfect gift, is at work to grow us to maturity, even in the midst of trials and suffering. How important to be reminded that the coming of the Lord is at hand and that we are to be wholehearted in following Him as we wait. And how timeous the reminder that we are part of the community of faith, that everyone matters, and that it is both our privilege and responsibility to love and to serve our brothers and sisters in Christ, even – and perhaps especially – when their own faith is weak. I am certainly grateful for the community of believers at St James Church, Kenilworth, with whom it has been my privilege, in easier times than these, to study this great letter. I trust that this present work will be an encouragement to them.

I am grateful to the Proclamation Trust for the invitation to contribute another volume to a series which has been such a great blessing to me and to many whose exquisite burden it is to preach to God's people week after week. My thanks to Jon Gemmell for his constant encouragement for the task and for his editorial work in adding clarity and readability to the work. Thanks also to David Jackman and Nigel Styles who offered constructive criticism of the manuscript and whose suggestions have meant a better end product. Words cannot express how thankful I am to my beloved wife Alison for her patience, support and prayers.

May God, the Father of our Lord Jesus Christ, who brought us forth by the word of truth, grant us deep understanding of the letter of James. And may He enable us to preach it with clarity and conviction for the good of His people and the glory of His name.

MERVYN ELOFF
Cape Town
May 2020

SERIES PREFACE

At first reading the letter of James can seem a bit like a blog, an assortment of James' musings on various aspects of the Christian life. However, dig a bit deeper and a unified, compelling and ferociously contemporary exhortation soon surfaces. James, far from being scattergun in his approach, writes with a unified theme and a unified purpose in order to bolster the resolve of his readers (and us) to live as wholehearted, single-minded, maturing and devoted disciples of the Lord Jesus. It is a message that 2000 years later has lost none of its urgency and none of its challenge. Mervyn will prove an excellent guide to help you see the big picture and intricate detail of this much loved, though much misunderstood letter.

This volume like all in the series are written with the preacher, Bible teacher and Bible student in mind. Part One, the introductory section, contains lots of important information to help you get a handle on the book of James as a whole. It covers aspects like authorship, structure, melodic line and how to plan a preaching series. There is also lots of encouragement to give yourself to the task of preaching and teaching James.

Then, Part Two works through the book looking sequentially at the detail of individual passages. For each of these preaching units there is lots of help offered both on the specifics but also how each section fits into the letter as a whole. There are also some pointers as to the structure of the section, theme and aim sentences, sermon outline, application and introduction. Each of the chapters finishes with help in writing a Bible study on the verses in view. The sections of Part Two are not written to take the hard work of preparation but to be a helping hand as you invest your time, efforts and gifts in prayerful preparation in order to teach the book of James to others.

Teaching James brings the number of published volumes in this series to twenty-five. From the comments we hear from people involved in regular preaching and Bible teaching ministry, we are encouraged by how well this series is developing. We long for these books to help people to keep working hard at the Word in order that they might proclaim the unsearchable riches of Christ ever more clearly.

Our thanks as always go to Christian Focus for their continued partnership in this project. Without their faith, expertise, servant-heartedness, enthusiasm and patience, none of these books would ever make it into your hands or onto your bookshelf.

JONATHAN GEMMELL &
DAVID JACKMAN
Series Editors
London 2021

How to Use This Book

Teaching James is written to help the preacher or Bible teacher understand the central aim and purpose of the text in view, to both deepen their own understanding and assist them in preaching and teaching it to others. Unlike a commentary, therefore, it does not go into exhaustive exegetical detail. Instead it helps us to engage with the theme and purpose of the letter of James, keeping the big picture in view and helping us see how to present the material to our hearers.

'Part One: Introducing James', lays the groundwork for the book as a whole. It helps us get up to speed with the author, occasion, purpose and structure of the letter. All the necessary ingredients one needs to ascertain before embarking on more detailed study of individual passages. Part One also offers some suggestions as to how to construct a sermon series on the book of James and why preaching and teaching James should be a vital part of a balanced spiritual diet.

'Part Two: Teaching James', looks at each of the individual preaching units suggested in Part One. The structure of each of these chapters is the same. It begins with an introduction to the passage followed by a section entitled 'Listening to the text', that outlines the structure, context and content of the unit, helping the reader to see what is there. All good biblical preaching begins with careful, detailed listening to the text and this is true for James as much as any other book.

After 'Listening to the text', comes a section called 'From text to message'. This offers suggestions as to the main theme and aim of the passage in view and then some skeleton outlines. These suggestions are nothing more than that – suggestions designed to help the preacher think about his own divisions of the text, structure of his sermon and clarifying the big idea of the passage. We are great believers in every preacher doing the hard work on the text themselves, because sermons need to flow first and foremost from our personal encounter with God in the text. Downloading other people's sermons or trying to breathe life into someone else's work are strategies doomed to failure. They may produce a reasonable talk, but in the long term, they are disastrous for the preacher himself since he needs to live in the word and the word to live in him, if he is to speak from the heart of God to the hearts of his congregation. These sections of Part Two are merely offered as grist for the mill and a helping hand to overcome inertia in the study.

Each chapter in Part Two concludes with some suggested questions for a group Bible study. These are grouped into two different types: questions to help *understand* the passage and questions to help *apply* the passage. Again these are not here simply to be copied and reproduced for your own Bible studies, but are offered as a helping hand as you prepare your own studies. All good Bible studies should drive participants to wrestle with the text and aim at everyone understanding the content more fully. Scripture should always be the focus rather than speculation, personal experience or individual's feelings.

Though written primarily for the preacher and Bible teacher, using this volume for individual study will also yield great fruit as you read the book of James for yourself. The detail, insights and help offered will aid you in getting a better grip on this dynamic little letter and hopefully having heard its message more clearly, by God's grace you will be enabled to live as a wholehearted, single-minded, devoted disciple of the Lord who shows their faith in every sphere of life.

However you use this book, our prayer is that it might assist you in understanding the book of James and when opportunity arises to teach it clearly, faithfully and compellingly to others.

Part One:

INTRODUCING JAMES

1.

Getting Our Bearings
in James

Introduction

Anyone setting out to preach through a New Testament letter must answer three basic but important questions: What does the text say? How does the text say what it says? Why does the text say what it says in the way that it says it?

The *what* and the *how* questions have to do with content, form and style. These questions can generally be answered by a close reading and careful exegesis of the text itself. They are vital questions as they enable the preacher to align the content and more particularly the emphasis of the sermon with the author's argument and emphasis. These questions also ensure that each individual sermon tracks with the overall message of the letter. Answering them takes time and hard work, but such labour brings valuable fruit and great satisfaction. Although the *what* and *how* questions are touched on in our discussion here in Part One of this book, they are dealt with in greater detail in Part Two.

The *why* question has to do with the aim or purpose of the text. Speaking personally this is often the most difficult of the three questions to answer with any kind of certainty. There are of course times when the author has provided clues as to aim or purpose as for example in 1 John 1:4, Jude 3 and John 20:30-31. But even where the purpose has been stated, more work needs to be done in order to piece together the specific situation into which the letter was sent. It is here that discussions about the date, authorship and provenance of the letter in commentaries and reference works are of real value. Even where the conclusions drawn are quirky, they provide 'grist for the mill' and force one to read the text more carefully, keeping the *why* question in mind. And this is the rich ground from which good application flows. So then, to questions of date, authorship, aim and purpose.

When and by whom was the letter written?

The letter of James begins with the traditional formula: (1) author, (2) recipients and (3) greeting. The author is described as 'James, a servant of God and of the Lord Jesus Christ'. Although various options have been proposed, especially in more recent times, the traditional view (assumed in this book) is that the author is James, the half-brother of the Lord and the leader of the Jerusalem church. As far as the rest of the New Testament is concerned, this James is known to us by name from the Gospels (Matthew 13:55 and Mark 6:3), the book of Acts (Acts 12:17; 15:13-21; 21:18) and from Paul's references to him in 1 Corinthians (15:7) and Galatians (1:19 and 2:9). Given James' scepticism about Jesus reported in the Gospels (see Mark 3:21 and John 7:5), it seems that like Paul, James came to faith through an encounter with the risen Lord Jesus Christ. Contrary to the suggestion of some, there is nothing at all in the New Testament accounts to suggest that he was at loggerheads with Paul, or that he had a particularly legalistic view of the Christian faith. Indeed, there is nothing in his letter to suggest that James was anything other than an orthodox and deeply committed follower of the Lord Jesus Christ. James' chief aim in writing as he did was to urge fellow believers for whom he had a pastoral concern, to resist the pressure of the world and to remain wholehearted themselves.

As far as the date of the letter is concerned, the following can be said: First, if James the brother of the Lord is the author of the letter, writing in his capacity as leader of the Jerusalem church, then enough time must have elapsed for him to have risen to such an important position. Furthermore, this seems likely only after Peter had left Jerusalem (Acts 12:17). Luke's description of Peter's departure comes in a chapter that focuses attention on Herod Agrippa, his persecution of the church, his execution of James the son of Zebedee (Acts 12:2) and Herod's own death (Acts 12:23). James the son of Zebedee was executed in A.D. 44 and Herod died that same year. Thus, Peter's departure and James' accession to the role of leading the Jerusalem church can be dated to that time, and therefore James' letter came after A.D. 44.

Second, if we concede the accuracy of Josephus' claim that James was martyred *circa* A.D. 61 or 62, then the letter must have been written earlier.

Third, if we bear in mind that the Judean famine was at its height in A.D. 46, and that the Council of Jerusalem took place in A.D. 48, these two events seem to frame the provenance of this letter. The references to trials, particularly of a socio-economic nature (e.g. James 1:9; 2:14-17), would fit well in the context of the famine and its immediate aftermath. Furthermore, although an argument from silence, some commentators have pointed to a lack of reference to the issues which were discussed and resolved at the council of Jerusalem. This suggests a date before A.D. 48. Taking all of this into consideration, we can tentatively deduce that the letter was written in A.D. 46 or 47.

Why was the letter written?

The introductory formula describes the recipients of the letter as 'the twelve tribes in the Dispersion' (James 1:1). We will return to this verse in detail in Part Two of this book, but for the moment we note that such a description of the recipients suggests a Jewish and, more particularly, a Jewish-Christian audience. The closest parallel to this greeting is 1 Peter 1:1, though on closer examination the differences are greater than the similarities. Indeed, at a verbal level the only thing they have in common is the word 'dispersion'. This raises an important question: What did the word 'dispersion', used traditionally by Judean Jews to describe those living outside of the land (see e.g. John 7:35), have to do with James' audience?

One answer to this question may be to say that James, like Peter, is writing to Jewish Christians living outside of Judea. Jewish Christians who had been converted through the preaching of Christian missionaries such as Paul, Silas and Barnabas. Certainly, Peter's reference to Pontus, Galatia, Cappadocia, Asia and Bithynia (1 Peter 1:1) points in that direction, and James' use of the more general description 'To twelve tribes in the Dispersion' does not contradict this view. If we compare James' phrase 'in the Dispersion' with the phrase 'into the Dispersion' used by Jerusalem Jews in John 7:35, then the case seems to be made that the first readers of this letter were located outside of Judea. And this certainly is the predominant view among commentators. But there is another aspect of the phrase 'in the Dispersion', its bearing on James' audience and therefore the purpose of his letter, that is worth noting, especially if we consider the early date of the letter.

According to Acts 8:1-4, Stephen's execution in Jerusalem led to a scattering (literally, 'dispersion') of believers from Jerusalem throughout the regions of Judea and Samaria. Though the verb in Acts 8 does not equate to the summary term 'the Dispersion', it does suggest that the experience of the early Judean believers was an 'exile' experience, a 'driving out' from their place of belonging by those who were in power and hostile to the true faith. Tragically and ironically, this came not at the hands of some foreign power like Assyria or Babylon or even Rome, but at the hands of their own countrymen.

The book of Acts makes clear that such a dispersion was instrumental in the spread of the gospel, but it would have created a major socio-economic problem for those who were dispersed. They would have been cut off from the community support that characterised the Jerusalem church in the early days (Acts 2:42-47; 4:32-37). Added to this it is likely that, for a good number of these early believers, support from the extended family would not have been forthcoming. Their conversion to Jesus the Nazarene would have been taken as an act of betrayal, a relational, if not literal, death sentence.

How vulnerable such a group would have been. Like many, they would have been dependent on day labour for survival. But they would also have been especially at risk of exploitation by hostile and unscrupulous landowners and merchants whose greed and lack of social conscience was so characteristic of the period leading up to the civil war and the destruction of Jerusalem in A.D. 70 (cf. the stinging, indeed prophetic rebuke against the 'rich' in James 5:1-6.) Imagine the pressure that these dispersed believers would have felt as the economic hardship and hostility grew on a daily basis. How attractive the way of the world might seem at such moments (cf. James 4:4). How tempting it must have been to compromise just to get by or to provide for one's family. And, how easy it would have been to fall into the trap of showing special favour to any believer with financial means, or, if one was part of the privileged few, of expecting 'royal treatment' as a potential benefactor of the church (cf. James 2:1-13). Imagine the temptation to cling to the little (or lots) one had, as 'insurance' against even tougher times (cf. James 2:14-17). And imagine the growing potential for conflict within the community in such times of stress, as harsh and angry words were spoken, and unexpressed, deep-seated attitudes of jealousy and bitterness rose to the surface (cf. James 4:1-10).

Of course, important as attention to historical context is for exegesis, it is vital to remember that our own attempts to recreate such a context must remain tentative and open to re-evaluation as we study the text in detail. In my opinion however, the picture of James' original audience and their circumstances sketched above is not only plausible, but helpful, especially when it comes to applying what James says.

As we noted earlier one of the key tools in determining the *why* of a New Testament letter is to be on the lookout for any hints that the author gives. The risk here is that these hints are sometimes more in the eye of the beholder than in the mind of the author. But there are safeguards along the way, helpful tools in trying to discern an author's main emphasis or purpose. One of these tools, particularly relevant for James, is to pay careful attention to the beginning and end of the letter, in our case James 1:1 and James 5:19-20.

These verses will be dealt with more particularly in Part Two, but it is worth noting two things. First, there is James' self-designation as 'a servant of God and of the Lord Jesus Christ' (James 1:1). At first glance this seems to bespeak the humility of the author. However, if one bears in mind his Jewishness and his position as the leader of the church in Jerusalem, another possibility emerges. James clearly does not consider himself to be an apostle, but does he consider himself to be a prophet in the tradition of the 'prophets who spoke in the name of the Lord' (James 5:10)? Certainly, the title 'servant of God' as a Greek rendering of the Hebrew title *ebed YHWH* ('servant of the LORD') is suggestive.

Second, we note the reference to the restoration, or, to use James' language, the bringing back of the sinner from his wandering ways (James 5:19-20). Coming right at the end of the letter, this surely says something about James' own pastoral concern for his readers. As we shall see, they were certainly in danger of becoming 'double-minded' (literally, 'two-souled') amidst their trials. But we also note that this reference to restoration is near James' reference to Elijah and his powerful prayer. This will be explored more fully later, but it is suggestive at the very least. Could it be that James felt the same prophetic burden that Elijah felt, faced not with a double-minded nation but a double-minded church? Is this letter a clear and prophetic call to be wholehearted and undivided as a follower of Jesus Christ?

How is the letter structured?

Even a preliminary study of commentaries on James is enough to show that the question of the macrostructure is not so easily answered. Several alternatives have been suggested based variously on content, theme, grammar, literary genre or a combination of the above. These different structures have been well summarised in McKnight (2011: 47-55).

As regards preaching or teaching the letter, the process of identifying smaller units is of greater importance than drawing final conclusions about the structure of the letter as a whole. Analysing these smaller preaching or teaching units is important since the structure of the text reveals its emphasis, and in expository preaching the emphasis of the text should shape the message.

As with all New Testament letters, the text form of James is primarily discourse. Strategies for discerning structure in discourse include

- reading and rereading the letter;

- noting repeated words and themes;

- noting grammatical features such as main verbs (identifying statements, questions and commands) and link words that connect ideas or text units.

For our present purposes, the following points are worth noting:

- Most commentators agree that there are some clearly discernible, self-contained units within the letter. These include 1:1; 2:1-13; 2:14-26; 3:1-12; 4:13-5:6; 5:7-12 and 5:19-20.

- Several key words and themes are repeated throughout the letter. These function as a unifying principle for subunits that at first glance seem to be unconnected. Although these repetitions are listed by the major commentaries, it is preferable to notice them yourself by reading and rereading the letter.

- For the purposes of the present work, the repetition of the following key words and themes is worth noting:

  - trials/testing/temptation (1:2, 12, 13, 14)

  - steadfastness/perseverance (1:3, 4, 12, 25; 5:11)

  - blessed (1:12, 25; 5:11)

  - perfect/complete (1:4, 17, 25; 2:22; 3:2)

  - double-minded ('double-souled')/soul (1:8, 21; 5:20) and heart (1:26; 3:14; 4:8; 5:5, 8)

  - draw near (4:8 (twice)) and wander / bring back (5:19, 20)

  - desires (1:14, 15; 4:2)/passions (4:1, 3)

  - pure/purify/cleanse (1:27; 3:17; 4:8)

  - wisdom (1:5; 3:13, 15, 17)

  - the world (1:27; 2:5; 4:4 (twice))

- ○ the word (1:18, 21, 22, 23)/the law (1:25; 2:8, 9, 10, 11, 12; 4:11)
- ○ the truth (1:18; 3:14; 5:19)
- ○ faith (1:3, 6; 2:1, 5, 14, 17, 18, 20, 22, 24, 26; 5:15)/believe (2:19, 23)
- ○ works (1:25; 2:14, 17, 18, 20-22; 24-26; 3:13)
- ○ doers/do (1:22, 23, 25; 2:8, 12, 13 ('shown'), 19; 3:18 ('make'); 4:17; 5:15 ('committed'))
- ○ doubt (1:6)/sincere (3:17)/distinctions (2:4) (all the same root word)
- ○ judge/judgment/condemnation (2:4, 12, 13 (twice); 3:1; 4:11, 12 (twice); 5:9 (twice),12)
- ○ righteousness / justification (1:20; 2:21, 23, 24, 25; 3:17; 5:6, 16)
- ○ poor/rich (1:10, 11; 2:2, 3, 5, 6; 5:1)
- ○ lowly/humble/proud (1:9; 4:6, 10)/boast (1:9; 3:14; 4:16)

- James' preferred form of address to his audience is the phrase 'my brothers'. The phrase is used fifteen times, at times with the adjective 'beloved' (1:16, 19; 2:5), at times without the possessive pronoun 'my' (4:11; 5:7, 9, 10). McCartney (2009: 63) has shown that the phrase often functions as a 'discourse marker' to introduce a unit, though it does occasionally occur in the middle of a discussion (e.g. 3:10).

- Throughout the letter there are several short, pithy sayings (e.g. 1:20; 2:13, 26; 3:18; 5:16), as well as more expansive sayings (e.g. 1:12, 27; 2:5, 10; 3:12;

5:20). These aphorisms and longer proverbial sayings are what give the letter its wisdom character. They also serve as structural markers, often to end a section (see further the discussion in McCartney (2009: 63-65)).

- James makes frequent use of commands, questions and statements. These shape the way his audience thinks and motivates them in a desired course of action. New sections and subsections of the letter typically begin with a command (1:2, 13, 16, 19; 2:1; 3:1; 4:13; 5:1, 7, 12) or question (2:14; 4:1; 4:13) or a combination of both (3:13; 5:13, 19).

Based on these observations and following, at least in broad terms, the structure suggested by McCartney we will adopt the following as a preaching outline for James:

1:1	A Significant Greeting
1:2–12	The Path to Life
1:13–18	Facing Temptation
1:19–25	The Word-Shaped Life
1:26–27	True Religion
2:1–13	Seeing People God's Way
2:14–26	Faith That Saves
3:1–12	Words! Words! Words!
3:13–18	Wisdom for Life
4:1–10	Wholehearted Christianity
4:11–12	Whose World Is It Anyway?
4:13–17	God Willing!
5:1–6	Exposed!

5:7–12   Hopeful Perseverance

5:13–20   A Call to Spiritual Restoration

What is the melodic line of the letter?[1]

The discussion of the structure of James' letter leads logically to a discussion of the overall theme or 'melodic line' of the letter. The conviction which lies behind this discussion is that just as every song has a unique tune or melody, so every Bible book has a unique message. The task of the preacher is then to listen carefully to the text and to try to discern what this overall theme or message is. And then, of utmost importance for the task of expository preaching, to work out how a particular passage in the book relates to the message of the book as a whole. Thus in order to ensure that we teach each passage in line with the author's aim and purpose, we need to keep asking two closely connected questions – namely, 'What is the message of the whole book?' and 'How does this passage relate to the message of the whole book?' This is a vital part of the process of exegesis and helps to do two things. First it safeguards the preacher against taking a passage out of its context and using it in a way that does not align with the author's intention. Second it enables the preacher to hear and teach the author's particular emphasis. Paying attention to the melodic line thus helps us to be both faithful and fresh in our preaching.

---

1. The use of the phrase 'melodic line' to talk about the overall theme or message of a Bible book goes back to the early preaching workshops run by Dick Lucas. The summary statement of the principle in this present work is taken with permission from the instructional outlines produced by the Charles Simeon Trust. See www.simeontrust.org

As with the task of identifying the main theme and aim of a particular passage, certain strategies can be used for identifying the melodic line of a book. These include: (1) reading and re-reading; (2) paying attention to the beginning and end of the book (top and tail); (3) finding purpose or thesis statements; (4) noting repeated words, phrases and ideas and (5) identifying the macro-structure of the book. Based on the outcome of these strategies a concise, provisional statement of the melodic line can be produced. This must then be re-evaluated and adjusted in the light of detailed work on each text. Speaking personally, I have found it helpful to try to express the melodic line in terms of both theme and purpose (see below).

Given the richness and diversity of the content of James' letter, the task of identifying a melodic line for the letter is quite demanding. On the one hand, one is tempted to define it too broadly so that it becomes little more than a summary of various themes. On the other hand, one can become reductionistic and end up ignoring important material. My own method has been to begin with the top and tail of the letter (1:1-12 and 5:7-20) in order to arrive at a preliminary statement of melodic line and then to refine that statement in the light of James' teaching in the body of the letter itself.

First, comparing 1:1-12 with 5: 7-20, we note that steadfastness under trial (1:12; 5:11) is part of James' key concern for his readers. We could then express a preliminary melodic line as follows:

James has written to Christians facing various kinds of trials to challenge and encourage them to remain steadfast to the end.

Second, we note the repetition of the word 'blessing' (1:12; 5:11) and the focus on prayer (1:6; 5:13-18). If we include this, we could modify our provisional melodic line as follows:

> James has written to Christians facing various kinds of trials to challenge and encourage them to remain prayerful and steadfast to the end. In doing so they will enjoy God's blessing and finally receive the gift of crown of life.

Certainly many of James' other themes such as the need for God's wisdom (1:5; cf. 3:13-18) and the nature of saving faith (1:2; cf. 2:14-26) can be seen to relate to this overarching concern for prayerful and steadfast perseverance.

Third, when we look more closely at 1:1-12, we note James' contrast between the 'perfect and complete' man (1:4) and the 'double-minded' man (1:8). This would suggest that being a double-minded man will undermine one's growth to maturity ('perfect' in context cannot mean sinless but should rather be understood as 'mature'). The double-minded man will be compromised when it comes to steadfastness and prayerful perseverance to the end. Fourth, when we look more closely at 5:7-20, we note James' exhortation about the importance of 'bringing back' someone who has wandered away from the truth (5:19-20). Rhetorically, this exhortation serves to create sympathy for those who are drifting and is intended to motivate the readers to action.[2] It is thus equivalent to a purpose statement, explaining one of the reasons why the letter was written.

---

2. In Ancient Rhetoric, the term for this kind of summary exhortation is *peroratio*.

This focus on the danger of double-mindedness and the importance of bringing back those who have wandered away is James' particular contribution to the theme of prayerful perseverance to the end. But should it be included in a statement of the melodic line? To answer this question, we need to look beyond the top and tail of the letter, to other literary features. And in this connection, James 4:4-10 is of particular importance.[3]

Even a cursory read through the letter shows that James uses a large number of imperatives, both negative and positive. This is particularly the case in 4:4-10. Furthermore, in this passage James replaces his customary form of address 'brothers' with the word 'adulterers'. As we shall see in our discussion of this text in Part Two, James is drawing on Old Testament language and imagery at this point and for good reason. For the moment we note that the blunt form of address and the multiplication of imperatives suggests that we have reached what Moo calls 'the emotional climax of the letter' (Moo: 2000,45-46). This then suggests that the problem of double-mindedness (4:8) and in particular, the call to repent of such double-mindedness and to return to wholehearted faith and commitment to the Lord is a central concern in the letter.

Taking the above observations into account then, we could summarise our understanding of the melodic line of the letter as follows:

James has written to Christians facing various kinds of trials:

---

3. See Douglas Moo's excellent discussion of the importance of 4:4-10 in discerning James' central concern (Moo:2000,45-46). My own conclusions are influenced by his valuable insight.

(1) to warn them against the danger of double-mindedness

(2) to urge them to repentance and wholehearted commitment to the Lord

(3) to remind them of God's blessing and His promise of the crown of life

(4) to remind them of their pastoral responsibility for those who are weak in the faith and in danger of wandering away so that they will remain prayerful and steadfast to the end and help others to do the same.

All that remains then is to express this in terms of a brief statement of melodic line such as

> James has written to those facing trials to turn them from double-mindedness to wholehearted, persevering faith and commitment to the Lord and to urge them to do the same for those who are in danger of wandering away.

2.

Why Should We Preach and Teach James?

How do the words of a first-century Jewish Christian leader written to first-century Jewish Christians apply to us today? That is the big question we face as we approach James' letter to the 'twelve tribes in the Dispersion'. It is important to affirm that this is a question about significance and application, not a question about meaning. Our conviction is that James' letter means today what it meant to the original hearers and that it is possible through proper exegesis to arrive at that meaning. But we do recognise – indeed we must recognise – that the circumstances in which we read the letter differ from those of the original audience and differ from reader to reader today. And yet, as we examine the message of James' letter more closely, we are reminded that we have a great deal in common with our first-century brothers and sisters in Christ. As we engage in rigorous exegesis it is amazing how potent and contemporary the message of James to *them then* is for *us now*.

First, we are reminded that, like them, we live in a fallen world where we face trials of various kinds. Furthermore, we are reminded that these trials are an opportunity for our spiritual growth to maturity. These trials are a means that God uses to grow our faith and not a sign that our faith is in some way lacking. This is surely an important message to hear today, given the ongoing influence of those who preach a triumphalist gospel, often to the great discouragement of ordinary believers.

Second, we are reminded that, like them, we are a fallen and sinful people, as susceptible to the pull of the world and the desires of our sinful hearts as they were. Like them, we need to be warned against double-mindedness. We too need to be told that we cannot and must not try to cultivate friendship with the world while at the same time claiming to be servants of God. God is one and we too need to hear and obey James' impassioned call to wholeheartedness in our own relationship with God in Christ. If nothing else James reminds us that Christianity is first and foremost a heart religion.

Third, we are reminded that because Christianity is a heart religion, it is also a practical religion. One of the hallmarks of James' letter is its use of imperatives and its focus on the importance of doing as well as hearing the Word, pointing us to the practical dimension of true faith. James gives many examples of this faith in action, most notably in the way we speak to and about people, and the way we treat people. In a world still characterised by prejudice and discrimination, dominated by materialism, and notorious for the thoughtless and sometimes harsh way words are used, we do well to listen to James. Then, having listened and with repentant and humble hearts, to speak and act in a way that is consistent with our claim to be followers of Christ, the Lord of glory.

Fourth, we are reminded that today as then, God is at work in the world according to His purpose of saving a people for His own possession, in this world and on the last day. James tells us that salvation comes by regeneration, repentance and faith in Christ. He calls us to humbly receive God's implanted word of life and to persevere in believing and doing that word. James also reminds us that we belong to the family of faith and that we are our brothers' and our sisters' keeper. As God's people we should do everything in our power through prayer and the word, not only to persevere ourselves but also to encourage others to persevere. We must strengthen those who are weak. We must seek by God's grace to bring back those who have lost their way and are beginning to wander away from the faith. This was one of the primary reasons James wrote his letter and is why it remains important for us today.

3.

Ideas for a Preaching or Teaching Series in James

Despite the letter's brevity, the task of preaching or teaching James is by no means straightforward. Even a quick overview of the letter shows a rich diversity of topics and a tantalising complexity in literary structure. The use of repetition and link words and the sermonic style of some parts of the letter give it a wisdom feel and suggest that attempts to trace a central theme are doomed to fail. This is perhaps one reason why systematic exposition of the whole letter is rare in comparison to short, thematic series on specific topics within the book. And, even if one grants that James 5:19-20 reveals the author's purpose in writing, it takes hard work and careful thought to see how the theme of spiritual restoration flows through the different parts of the letter. Furthermore, careful study shows that, although James has deep theological convictions, these are not presented in traditional form and must be gleaned piecemeal while reading the letter. And, of course, some find James' Christology particularly thin, so hard work needs to be done to ensure that the letter is preached not merely as moral wisdom but as Christian scripture.

And yet, as we noted above, James' letter is of immense value and importance for the church. And so, despite the challenges that emerge along the way, committing to teaching or preaching a series in this letter is a very worthwhile and rewarding exercise.

Option 1: A series of consecutive expositions

Given James' relative brevity and underlying coherence of theme, a series of consecutive expositions through James seems to be both manageable and optimal. A series based on the analysis used in this book would take about fifteen weeks. This series can be summarised as seen below (see each passage in Part Two for a more detailed breakdown).

Undivided: An exposition of the Letter of James

Sermon 1	'A Significant Greeting'	1:1
Sermon 2	'The Path to Life'	1:2-12
Sermon 3	'Facing Temptation'	1:13-18
Sermon 4	'The Word-Shaped Life'	1:19-25
Sermon 5	'True Religion'	1:26-27
Sermon 6	'Seeing People God's Way'	2:1-13
Sermon 7	'Faith That Saves'	2:14-26
Sermon 8	'Words! Words! Words!'	3:1-12
Sermon 9	'Wisdom for Life'	3:13-18
Sermon 10	'Wholehearted Christianity'	4:1-10
Sermon 11	'Whose World Is It Anyway?'	4:11-12
Sermon 12	'God Willing!'	4:13-17
Sermon 13	'Exposed!'	5:1-6
Sermon 14	'Hopeful Perseverance'	5:7-12
Sermon 15	'A Call to Spiritual Restoration'	5:13-20

As we noted in the introductory comments, in a longer series of consecutive expositions care must be taken to ensure that each exposition is aligned to the author's overall aim in the letter. As the series title *Undivided* states, that main aim is to challenge believers to persevere in the face of trials and temptations, remaining steadfast, undivided and wholehearted in their loyalty to God and their faith in Him. It remains important, however, to let each text speak its own message as part of the whole, without flattening out the contours or individual emphases of any one text.

Option 2: Thematic studies

During his appeal for wholehearted devotion to the Lord, James engages with several important issues. James' didactic style also deals with these issues fairly comprehensively in each passage or in a series of related passages on a similar topic. Such issues can be dealt with in single talks or a short series, rather than as part of a long series of consecutive expositions. Indeed, each of the talks listed above as part of the expository series could be given as a single talk on the specific topic which is in focus in the passage.

Such single talks or shorter series give an opportunity for a more wide-ranging treatment of the issue raised in each text. But care should be taken against preaching 'framework' rather than text. To avoid such 'framework preaching' two important points must be kept in mind. First, it remains important to stick to that aspect of the issue that James in fact deals with in a particular text. This means that James' distinctive contribution on a particular subject will be heard. Second, each text should be interpreted and thus taught in line with rather than independently of the overall theme or melodic line of the letter. Attention to these two points will ensure that the preacher does not go beyond what is written, but rather lets the text speak in its own terms.

An example of such a thematic series, based on a number of texts from the letter, is outlined below.

The Christian and wealth

Talk 1: 'A Surprising Insight' (*Text: James 1:5-11*)

Here, following a general introduction to the subject and its importance, the talk would aim to show that wealth, like poverty, is a trial to be faced with the wisdom that God gives. Furthermore, and in keeping with James' overall concern, the connection with double-mindedness could be made by showing how different such a perspective is from that which the world in general has. Both the rich and the poor need God's wisdom if they are to respond to such trials in a godly rather than worldly way.

Talk 2: 'Seeing People God's Way' (*Text: James 2:1-13*)

Here the main aim of the talk would be to challenge the common tendency we have to favour the rich and powerful but disparage the poor. Such treatment of people is sadly all too common in our world today. But it is not the path that Christians are called to follow. God does not show favouritism and nor should we. Such behaviour is sin and a clear symptom of double-mindedness. It should not be tolerated among those who claim to follow the Lord.

Talk 3: 'The Problem With Greed' (*Text: James 4:1-10*)

Here the main aim of the talk would be to expose the problem of greed that haunts our hearts. Such greed is a clear expression of double-mindedness, a deadly idolatry that God hates. The only cure for greed is wholehearted repentance.

Talk 4: 'Perspective' (*Text: James 4:11-5:6*)

Here the main aim of the talk would be to show how worthless riches are when seen in the light of eternity. We leave everything behind when we die. The rich should neither be envied nor hated. They should in fact be pitied and indeed evangelised for they must stand before the throne of God the righteous judge and give an account to Him. And above all, those who follow the Lord should seek His grace and the power to have this perspective on wealth, for nothing is more destructive to a wholehearted relationship with the Lord than the love of money.

Part Two:

TEACHING JAMES

I.

A Significant Greeting
(James 1:1)

Introduction

Despite its brevity, James' opening greeting sets the tone for what is to follow. First, the greeting identifies the author and affirms his relationship with the Lord in whose name he writes. Second, the greeting reminds the audience of the spiritual privileges and the spiritual responsibilities that they have. Third, the greeting acknowledges the challenging circumstances of those to whom the letter is addressed and provides the context for the pastoral exhortation that follows in the rest of the letter.

Listening to the text

Context and structure

As noted in Part One, the letter of James begins with the traditional formula: (1) author, (2) recipients and (3) greeting. Although brief, this traditional formula contains important qualifying statements, about both the author and his audience. The words 'in the Dispersion' provide the theological and sociohistorical context for the discussion of 'trials' and 'temptations' in the rest of chapter 1. The word 'greetings' in verse 1 is verbally connected to the word 'joy' in verse 2. This is the first of a number of instances where James uses repeated 'link' words to transition between sections or to connect paragraphs and ideas with each other.

Working through the text

The author begins his letter by describing himself as a 'servant of God and of the Lord Jesus Christ'. Comparison with the introductory formulae of other New Testament letters shows this self-designation to be unique. Only Paul introduces himself as a 'servant of God' as James does, but then immediately follows that introduction with the words 'and an apostle of Jesus Christ' (Titus 1:1), a title that James cannot and does not use. Paul describes himself as 'a servant of Christ Jesus' (Rom. 1:1) and Jude describes himself as 'a servant of Jesus Christ' (Jude 1), but neither context contains a reference to being 'a servant of God'. James alone refers to himself as a servant both of God and of the Lord Jesus Christ.

What are we to deduce from James' description of himself in this particular way? Certainly, as most commentators observe, James' reference to himself as a servant speaks of an appropriate humility, both before God and before the Lord Jesus Christ. Such humility before God was to be expected of a devout Jew, but James' acknowledgement of Jesus as 'the Lord' whose servant he now is, is particularly striking. Such an acknowledgement presupposes not merely a dramatic but a miraculous change of mind with respect to Jesus (see John 7:5). As we noted in Part One, this change was in all likelihood due to James' encounter with the risen Lord Jesus, though we note James' inclusive language in describing how God 'brought us forth by the word of truth' (James 1:18). From this we can surely deduce that James' conversion was on the basis not only of an encounter with the risen Lord but also through hearing the word of truth, the gospel 'in accordance with the Scriptures' (cf. 1 Cor. 15:3-4). Nor should we miss the theological significance of the conjunction in this statement. In describing himself as a servant of God *and* of the Lord Jesus Christ, James ascribes the highest possible authority and dignity to Jesus, an authority and dignity equal to that of the Father. Here then, almost in passing, we find evidence that belief in the deity of Christ was not a later addition to Christian doctrine but something held as foundational to the faith from earliest times.

While many commentators point out that a position of service before God carried with it a sense of dignity and authority, there is a prophetic element contained in the title 'servant of God' that they largely ignore. In Old Testament terms Moses was the 'servant of God' par excellence (see e.g. Exodus 14:31; Deuteronomy 34:5; 1 Kings 8:53). But the term is also used of the Old Testament prophets in general, especially in relation to the LORD's patience in sending prophets to call Israel to return to the LORD (see especially 2 Kings 17:13 and Jeremiah 7:25). Given James' own Jewish identity and the description of his audience as 'the twelve tribes in the Dispersion', it may well be that in describing himself as 'a servant of God and of the Lord Jesus Christ' James is claiming prophetic authority for his message. This case will I trust become clearer as we explore James' message in the letter as a whole.

James' description of his audience as 'the twelve tribes in the Dispersion' is worthy of exploration. As we noted in Part One, the dispersion that is in view here is probably that dispersion of Jewish believers from Jerusalem into Judea and Samaria following the death of Stephen (Acts 8:1).

As a matter of historical fact, the ten northern tribes were dispersed with the fall of Samaria (*circa* 722 B.C.). These tribes remained dispersed, as the kingdom of Israel, founded by Jeroboam I, ceased to exist after that date. It is also clear from the books of Ezra and Nehemiah that many from the southern tribes of Judah and Benjamin declined or were unable to return under Zerubbabel after the exile in Babylon. Nevertheless, Old Testament prophetic eschatology had as its focus an Exodus-like restoration resulting not only in a restored Jerusalem and Davidic kingdom but also in a reunited Israel (see e.g. Isa. 43:1-7; 44:1-5; Hosea 1:10-11), with the twelve tribes brought back together as one people.

By referring to his Christian Jewish audience as the 'twelve tribes', it is clear that, from James' perspective, this restoration had already partially taken place through the Lord Jesus Christ. James 2:1 makes clear that his audience are included, having come to faith. By speaking about them as 'dispersed', James makes clear that this physical dispersion signifies a partial and 'not yet' nature to this restoration. As believers in the Lord Jesus Christ, they and not the Jews had been given the privileges and the responsibilities of truly belonging to the people of God. But their restoration was not yet complete, nor would it be until the return of the Lord of glory, Jesus Christ (James 2:1; 5:7-9). As the people of God therefore they were called to faith, to brotherly love and to patient endurance.

They were to take care that neither they nor their fellow believers were polluted by the world (1:27) or wandered away from the truth (5:19-20). It was thus with prophetic authority and pastoral concern and also as a fellow believer in the Lord Jesus Christ that James wrote his letter and made his appeal.

From text to message

The question of the importance and relevance of the book of James as a whole (see Part One) is of course particularly pertinent when it comes to the introductory greeting of the letter. Is it really worth preaching a sermon on this first verse, or should you just jump straight to the meatier section dealing with trials and perseverance? Three reasons would suggest that time spent on the introductory greeting is a worthwhile exercise.

First, the summary of James' credentials is an opportunity for us to be reminded that the letter comes to us as the word of God and with the authority of the Lord Jesus Christ. What James said to his first audience is what the Lord said to them and continues to say to us today. We do well to bear this in mind even when what James writes challenges our way of thinking or our conduct.

Second, the focus on both the privileges and challenges of life as believers still 'in the Dispersion' gives us the chance to reflect on the reality of the 'now/not yet' of every Christian's experience. We may be the redeemed, privileged people of God, sharing this privilege with these early Jewish believers (see Acts 11:15-18). However, like them, we are still waiting for the fullness of God's kingdom rule. Like them, we face the challenges of life in a fallen world as we wait for the return of our Lord and saviour

Jesus Christ. Thus, this element of the greeting reminds us of just how relevant the letter is for our Christian lives and how important it is for our godliness. For in the midst of a fallen world the most important thing of all is that we hear and live by the word of God in Scripture.

Third, the miracle of grace evident in James' own life is surely worth noting. As with Paul, the move from unbelief to faith through an eye-witness encounter with the risen Lord (see above) was dramatic and is not the norm for us. And yet, as Paul himself testifies, such grace shown to sceptics and opponents is a reminder that anyone can indeed be saved and that we too may find our place in service of King Jesus (cf. 1 Tim. 1:16).

Getting the message clear: the theme
God, through James, has spoken and still speaks an authoritative and relevant word for His people living in the midst of a fallen and often hostile world.

Getting the message clear: the aim
To encourage and challenge believers to hear, receive and obey what James writes in his letter as the very word of God, a word for us today.

A way in
Given that a sermon on James 1:1 would aim to introduce the series as a whole, the best way in would probably be to highlight the reality of our present Christian experience. It is an experience that we share with James' original audience. On the one hand we are privileged people, chosen by the Lord and redeemed by Christ. On the other hand, we live in a fallen world and do not yet enjoy the full blessings of Christ's rule. There is thus a 'now' and a 'not yet' element

to our Christian experience. Two questions could then be asked by way of introduction:

- Question 1: 'What pressures do we face under such circumstances?' Answer: 'Pressure to doubt and compromise, perhaps even to "turn back" from wholehearted following of Jesus.'

- Question 2: 'What do we need more than anything else if we are to stand firm under such circumstances?' Answer: 'A clear and reliable word from God to encourage us and to help us to stand firm and wholehearted in our commitment to Christ. This clear and reliable word is exactly what James' letter provides for us.'

Ideas for application

- The authentic Christian life is a 'now/not yet' experience.

- James' letter provides us with an authoritative and relevant word from God to help us stand firm as we live for Christ in a fallen, hostile world.

Suggestions for preaching

Sermon

As noted in Part One, given my understanding of the melodic line of James, I have chosen *Undivided* as a title for the sermon series. This series title will be used for each sermon outline throughout the book.

Undivided (Talk 1)

'A Significant Greeting' (James 1:1)

1. Introduction

- The reality of our experience:
  - The privilege we enjoy
  - The pressure we face
  - The need we have

2. Our common faith:

- The twelve tribes – a privileged people of God
  (We share a common faith with first-century Jewish believers. Thus, the spiritual privilege that we enjoy is precisely the same as the privilege they had – the privilege of being God's chosen people.)

- In the Dispersion – an opposed people living in a fallen world
  (Like the first-century believers, we face opposition for our faith, and that can cause us to doubt our faith or perhaps just grow cold in our commitment to Jesus. Furthermore, although we are believers, we are not spared from the everyday trials of life in a fallen world. This experience of trials and tribulations is part of the normal Christian life.)

3. God's good provision:

- A surprising messenger
  (Here there is an opportunity to speak about the change that God brought about in James' life.)

- An authoritative and relevant word
  (Here the focus is on James' self-designation as a servant of God and of the Lord Jesus Christ. In particular, this provides an opportunity to think about the authoritative nature of what James has to say and its particular relevance as a 'prophetic' word designed to keep us undivided in our walk with the Lord.)

Suggestions for teaching

Questions to help understand the passage

1. Compare James 1:1 with the introductory greetings of other New Testament letters.

   - What similarities or differences do you note?

   - In what way is James' introductory greeting unique?

2. How does James describe himself in relation to God?

3. Look up 2 Kings 17:13 and Jeremiah 7:25.

   - What word is used in these verses to describe the prophets?

   - According to these verses, what were the prophets sent to do?

   - What light do these verses cast on James' description of himself as a 'servant of God'?

4. How does James describe himself in relation to the Lord Jesus Christ? What is striking about this description?

5. What does James' description of first-century Jewish Christians as the 'twelve tribes' imply?

6. What does James mean when he refers to these believers as 'in the Dispersion'? (Compare this phrase with John 7:35 and Acts 8:1.)

Questions to help apply the passage

1. Look up Acts 11:15-18. According to this passage, what do believers today have in common with first-century believers, both Jewish and Gentile?

2. Given the common faith we share with first-century believers, what privileges do we enjoy as God's chosen people? (Look in particular at James' description of his audience as the 'twelve tribes'.)

3. James describes his first audience as 'in the Dispersion'. What does this phrase bring to mind?

4. How do you think the reality of life 'in the Dispersion' applies to Christians today?

5. James' letter was designed especially for Christians who, though privileged to belong to God, had their faith and their commitment tested through the challenge of living in a fallen and often hostile world. What relevance do you think James' letter may have for us?

6. Why should we listen to and obey James' teaching even when it challenges our way of thinking or our conduct?

2.
The Path to Life
(James 1:2-12)

Introduction

In James 1:2-12 we move from the introductory greeting to exhortation. We begin to hear James' deep concern for his readers as they grapple with the challenges of living as God's people in the midst of a fallen world. The focus of the passage is upon 'trials of various kinds' (1:2) and more particularly upon how to remain 'steadfast' (1:3, 4, 12) in the face of such trials. Comparison with Romans 5:1-5 and 1 Peter 1:3-9 shows that James is not alone in helping believers understand trials and teaching them how to respond correctly. But as closer examination and comparison of each of these passages shows, each writer brought their own perspective to the question. For James, trials of various kinds are a God-ordained and essential element in the process by which believers grow to be 'perfect and complete' – that is, mature, single-minded, wholehearted followers of the Lord Jesus. The trials of this present life are to be seen from God's point of view with the wisdom that God gives. Though hard, they are to be faced, by faith, with steadfastness and, by God's good grace, with joy.

Listening to the text

Context and structure

As noted above, the transition from the introductory greeting to the body of the letter comes via a play on the words 'greetings' (v. 1) and 'joy' (v. 2). The imperative 'Count it all joy' and the more personalised form of address 'my brothers' in verse 2 make it clear that a new section of the letter has begun. The decision to treat 1:2-12 as a unit does however require some justification.

First, one must admit that much can be said for including 1:12 with what follows rather than with what precedes, particularly since 'trial' (1:12) and 'tempted' (1:13) are the same word in the original, and the contrast between the promise of 'life' (1:12) and the threat of 'death' (1:15) can be taken as a thematic bracket for the subsection 1:12-15.

However, the repetition of the word for 'trial'/'tempt' could just as easily be explained in terms of James' use of link words to transition from one section to another, as in 1:1 to 1:2 ('greetings'/'joy') and in 1:4 to 1:5 ('lacking'/'lacks'). Furthermore, it is worth noting that the repetition of key words in 1:2-3 and 1:12 ('trials'/'trial'; 'steadfastness'/'steadfast'; 'testing'/'test') is even stronger than that between 1:12 and 1:13 ('trial'/'tempted'). This repetition does seem to suggest that 1:2-3 and 1:12 bracket a section. It is also worth noting that 1:12 is the first of the so-called proverbial sayings (see Part One), which generally serve to end sections and subsections of the text. This strengthens the view that 1:2-12 is a unified section of text.

Of course, any proposal about the structure and limits of the passage as a whole must account for the apparent change of theme in 1:5-8 and 1:9-11. The text in 1:5-8 is about trials, steadfastness and wisdom, whereas 1:9-11 addresses wealth and poverty. Were it not for 1:12, it could well be argued that 1:2-4, 1:5-8 and 1:9-11 form three quite distinct sections. However, if, as suggested above, 1:12 is the conclusion of the section begun in 1:2, then a logical explanation for linking 1:9-11 with 1:5-8 and 1:2-4 must be provided. It is here that the idea of God-given wisdom (1:5) is fundamental. In 1:9-11 James presents a radical perspective on wealth and poverty, viewing both as part of the socio-historical context of the letter and thus as a trial that must be faced with the wisdom that God gives.

Finally, bearing in mind that a key tool for discerning structure is the presence of key themes or ideas, it is important to note the contrast in the passage between the '*double-souled*', *unstable* man (1:8) and the *steadfast, perfect* man (1:4). The latter is in the final analysis the *blessed* man (1:12), the one who, persevering to the end, will receive 'the crown of life'. This not only strengthens the link between 1:2-4 and 1:5-8 but also suggests that the logic of the passage as a whole is driving the reader to the conclusion that James gives in 1:12. Thus the emphasis and the main idea of the passage can be summed up as setting out the true 'path to life'. It is a path one must follow through various trials, refusing the alternative paths on offer.

Working through the text

Face trials with steadfastness (1:2-4)

Having described his readers formally as 'the twelve tribes in the Dispersion' in his opening greeting, James now addresses them as his 'brothers' (1:2) (cf. 1:16, 19; 2:1, 14; 3:1, 10; 4:11; 5:7, 9, 10, 12, 19). This form of address, while not unusual in the New Testament letters, is worth noting in this letter, especially as there can be some ambiguity as to whom James has in mind. (See comments on 1:10 below.) Certainly, James' reference to his readers as 'brothers', or at times 'beloved brothers', serves to strengthen the idea of their common faith in one Heavenly Father (1:17; 1:27; 3:9) and their common obligation to express that faith in a way that is consistent with the Father's perfect purpose. It also places James' sometimes strong words of rebuke and warning within the context of the family of faith, casting them as the words of one member of the family who is deeply and rightly concerned about the others.

By the end of the letter it will have become clear that James' primary concern for his brothers in the faith is that they do not wander away from the truth. He thus begins by addressing the reality of 'trials of various kinds' (1:2), circumstances which, unless approached correctly, could cause his fellow believers to lose heart and turn away. The phrase 'trials of various kinds' is deliberately vague and general. However, the constant references to poverty and wealth in the letter, and the pointed reference to the oppression of the poor by the rich (2:6, 7), would suggest that the socio-economic challenges that the readers faced made up at least a significant part of these trials. James' use of the word 'when' (literally, 'whenever') in regard to facing trials suggests that such 'trials of various kinds' were bound to come along sooner or later in the life of every believer. In that sense 'trials of various kinds' were entirely consistent with a life of faith lived 'in the Dispersion'.

Although such trials could and did become the occasion
for temptation and sin (see 1:13-18), James wants his
readers to see them in a completely different light, namely
as an opportunity for training and growth to maturity. The
command 'Count it all joy . . . when you meet trials' (1:2)
was (and is) of course counterintuitive. The joy that James
is describing here is not the same thing as circumstantial
happiness, nor is it primarily a feeling. Rather, joy in this
context has to do with a faith response to trials. This joy
is a settled attitude of heart and mind, a course of action
that is based on what the believers know about how trials
function in God's purposes.

In appealing to his readers to respond in the right way
to trials, James reminds them of something that they
know. They know and must keep in mind (that is the force
of the present tense of the word 'know') that trials are sent
not to destroy faith but to test faith – that is, to purify
and strengthen faith (1:3). The way in which this happens
is simple and powerful. Trials cause believers to have to
persevere in their faith, to remain steadfast in faith (1:3).
And, over time, such perseverance in faith will produce
maturity in the believer so that he or she may indeed be
'perfect and complete, lacking in nothing.' Given what we
have said about the assumed economic struggle of many
of the believers to whom James writes, this latter phrase
would have been potent!

It is with this progress towards maturity in mind that
James does not simply state that steadfastness is a step
on the way to maturity but rather calls upon his readers
to 'let steadfastness have its full effect' (1:4). Literally,
James says, 'Let steadfastness do its perfect work'. Thus,
the *perfect* work of such steadfastness in the face of trials

is to produce the *perfect* believer. What such perfection is needs to be explored more fully in the light of the letter as a whole. At this point it is clear that it involves 'wholeness' or 'completeness' (1:4), which, as we will see, is the opposite of being 'double-souled' (see 1:8). If we connect the command to 'let steadfastness have its full effect' with the command to 'count it all joy when you face various kinds of trials', we are in a position to cast fresh light on what it might mean to count the facing of trials all joy. To count trials as joy is to see them in the light of God's perfect purpose. The believers, rather than seeking the easy way out of such trials by worldly compromise, are to respond to them as opportunities to grow their faith in the Lord and develop their character as true believers.

Ask God for wisdom (1:5-8)

In 1:2-4 James urges his readers to see trials not from a human perspective but from God's point of view. There is a spiritual logic to trials and thus a faithful way of responding to them. But James is well aware that such a perspective does not come naturally to people, even if they are true believers. He thus urges his readers to ask God for wisdom – that is, spiritual insight to understand and correctly respond to their circumstances. Such wisdom is, and can only be, a gift from God (1:5). More to the point, this God is the 'giving God', who 'gives generously to all without reproach' (1:5). The asker is thus urged to approach God confidently, 'in faith' (1:6), with the assurance that all who ask will receive (1:5).

There is however a subtle point here that we need to keep in mind. In urging his readers to ask God for wisdom, James is not suggesting that they will receive some kind of mystical insight or power to overcome their difficulties.

God's gift of wisdom is linked to 'faith' and also linked to God's 'word of truth' (cf. 1:17-18). God's true word regarding trials and their role in the life of the believer has already been addressed in 1:2-4. Therefore, the wisdom that believers are to seek is the ability to understand, accept and act upon the truth that James has already spelt out regarding trials and their God-ordained purpose.

The alternative to facing trials by approaching God 'in faith' (1:6) and asking for wisdom is to face various kinds of trials as 'one who doubts' (1:6). At first glance this doubt seems merely to be faith in two minds, akin to the father who prays, 'I believe; help my unbelief' (Mark 9:24). On closer examination however we note that the 'doubting' that James warns against is something rather more serious. In 1:8 the doubter is identified as a 'double-minded' (literally, 'double-souled') man. This is James' first reference to this kind of person and the assessment is not positive. First, the 'double-minded' man will not receive anything (1:7) from the giving God who gives to all! Second, the 'double-minded' man is 'unstable in *all* his ways' (1:8), a telling summary statement that explains the striking metaphor in 1:6, the first of many in the letter. Later in the letter, this double-minded man is described in even more chilling terms and is called upon not to exercise 'more faith' but to repent! (cf. 4:1-10). It would seem then that in 1:5-8 James is already laying the foundations for this call to repentance and beginning his appeal to those who are wandering away to turn back before it is too late.

A radical perspective (1:9-11)

As we noted above, one of the particular trials that James' readers faced was the challenge of thinking correctly about wealth and social status. Later in the letter this challenge is spelt out in practical terms, addressing favouritism and discrimination, charity, speech (especially judgmental words), pride, jealousy, anger and dissension. But in 1:9-11 James goes to the root problem behind this conduct and deals with the issue of Christian identity.

James identifies two groups, describing them in terms of their 'this world' status. On the one hand, we have 'the lowly brother' (1:9) – the believer who lacks material wealth and thus social status. On the other hand, we have 'the rich man' (1:10, 11). The parallelism in 1:9-10, plus the use of a single verb ('boast' in 1:9, also implied in 1:10), suggests that the word 'brother' must apply to both persons in question. We are thus dealing with a lowly brother and a rich brother, both of whom are called upon as believers to see themselves not as the world does but in the light of God's wise and true word. James' use of the word 'boast' in 1:9 seems, at first glance, out of place. The word is used elsewhere in the New Testament in a positive sense, especially in relation to the trials that believers face and the hope of glory that they have (e.g. Romans 5:1-5, where it is translated 'rejoice'). However, in James the word 'boast' is used in a negative sense in 3:14 and 4:16 (though a cognate word is used positively in 2:13, where it is translated 'triumphs over'). Thus it seems that James is using wordplay to reverse accepted ways of thinking and redefine them in the light of God's way of seeing the world.[1]

The 'exaltation' of the lowly brother is not so much that person's current spiritual status (though that is included

---

1. Note a similar wordplay occurs with the noun 'lowly' in 1:9 and the verb 'humble yourselves' in 4:10. We will discuss this wordplay and its reversal of perspective when we look at 4:1-10.

in the term 'brother') as their future hope as spelt out in 1:12. The lowly brother who remains steadfast in the faith is 'blessed' and will indeed 'receive the crown of life'. Thus, rather than dwelling on present inequalities, this brother is to fix his heart and mind on future hope. This does not mean that James is indifferent to poverty and struggle – quite the contrary, as the letter clearly shows. But he is concerned that circumstance met with human sinfulness may cause this brother to fall into double-mindedness, turning away from wholehearted devotion to the Lord. Thus he emphasises what they have in the Lord not what they lack in the world.

The 'humiliation' of the rich brother is explained by James in 1:10-11. Using language reminiscent of Isaiah 40:6-8, James reminds this brother that he will die and that material wealth in this world is no foundation for the life of the world to come. The rich, like everyone else, will 'fade away in the midst of his pursuits' (1:11). The hard truth that all of us will die is a God-given reminder that our wealth does not and must not define us. All that really matters in the end is the crown of life that God gives to those who love Him. In this life then the rich believer does well to remember his mortality and, in the light of it, to love the Lord with all his heart.

A striking conclusion (1:12)

As we noted in Part One, James frequently uses short, pithy sayings or longer proverbial sayings to end sections of the letter. James ends this first section with a clear statement designed to motivate his readers to act upon the wise counsel that they have been given. The aim of the entire section is to motivate them to remain steadfast in the face of various trials, knowing that such steadfastness in faith is what produces Christian maturity. In this concluding statement, James reminds them that such choices, though difficult, are a life and death matter and the road to life is via the pathway of trials, testing and steadfast perseverance. He also reminds them that the path of faith and steadfastness is not a mere duty but an expression of our love for God. This positive link between steadfastness and love mirrors the link between joy and steadfastness in 1:2-3.

James begins by pronouncing a blessing upon those who respond to trials with steadfast faith. In 1:25 he reminds those who hear and do the word that this is indeed the way of blessing. In 5:11 he reminds his readers that the prophets and saints of old like Job 'remained steadfast' and for this they were considered blessed. This suggests that 'blessed' means much more than happy or contented. A better way to think of the word is to see it as the Lord's verdict upon those who follow His way and remain upon the path. This implies that the word 'blessed' carries with it present approval as well as final vindication. In 1:12 the blessedness of the one persevering is therefore precisely the crown of life that they will receive from God.

The positive, motivational tone of this closing statement is underlined in two ways. First, James uses the word 'when' not 'if' to describe the one who has 'stood the test' brought about by trials. The word 'when' implies the certainty of reward for those who remain steadfast, and this very sense of certainty is surely positive motivation. James will issue stern warnings in the letter, but here the aim is to encourage and exhort his readers toward the best outcome. The certainty of the reward and thus the motivation for steadfastness is of course further underlined by James' reference to the crown of life as something which God has 'promised'.

From text to message

Contrary to the bold claims of the so-called New Atheists there is in fact a vast difference between fanatical religion and authentic Christianity. This difference can be seen in many ways, not least in the approach to trials and tribulations in daily life. From the point of view of fanaticism, trials are seen either as *validation* or as *disqualification*, either as essential or as contrary to God's will for His people.

James' insightful view on trials in the life of the believer is an important antidote to each of these errors and thus of great importance and relevance to us today. But in preaching 1:2-12, we can inadvertently fall into the very errors that James is seeking to counter. Thus, we should avoid preaching 'joy because of trials' rather than 'joy in the midst of trials'. We should avoid being reductionistic in defining trials. James speaks of 'trials of various kinds' and his example of *both* poverty *and* wealth as a trial is striking indeed. Furthermore, the word 'whenever' reminds us that at times we will not face trials and this fact does not mean that we have necessarily compromised. In fact, perhaps the most important thing to bear in mind in preaching this passage is that James' main emphasis is not on trials but on perseverance and steadfastness and on the importance of being wholehearted in our faith. Thus, the passage invites us to look to God in faith, love and hope and to see all of life, including our trials, from His perspective.

Getting the message clear: the theme

Trials are a reality of this fallen world and are part of the way in which God grows His people to maturity in the faith. Because this is true, we can trust God's goodness in allowing trials and ask God for wisdom so that we may remain steadfast in faith even in the midst of trials.

Getting the message clear: the aim

To encourage believers to see trials from a faith perspective – that is, from the point of view of God's good purpose and in the light of eternity.

To encourage believers not to lose heart but rather to persevere in faith even in the midst of trials.

A way in

One way in to preaching this passage could be to highlight the stark difference between fanatical religion and authentic Christianity, especially when it comes to dealing with trials. This then paves the way for shaping the sermon around James' realistic, balanced yet radical approach to trials.

Another way in could be to ask our hearers to think about their own response to trials and then to list a few common responses. For example, we might say that trials challenge our faith and cause us to doubt God's goodness or power. Or we may say that trials cause us to wonder if we have done something wrong to cause God to punish us. This then paves the way for showing that trials can and do befall all Christians. We can tell people that in God's power and goodness He uses trials to grow our faith not to destroy it. In the end, trials are temporary, but God's good work in our lives will last forever.

Ideas for application

- Trials come in various forms and are part of the normal Christian life.
- God uses trials to grow us to maturity.

- In the midst of trials, we are sometimes overcome with doubt.

- The right response to trials is to ask for God's wisdom to see trials correctly.

- As believers we are called to persevere in faith and remain steadfast.

- In the end, the trials of this present world will give way to the crown of life.

- God is faithful to His promises, and His purposes for us are always good.

Suggestions for preaching

Sermon

Undivided (Talk 2)

'The Path to Life' (James 1:2-12)

1. Introduction: a stark contrast
   - A fanatic's view of trials
   - A Christian's view of trials

2. Seeing trials God's way (1:2-4)
   - The normality of trials

     (Trials are part of the normal Christian life and do not invalidate our faith. However, trials do not necessarily authenticate our faith. They are in fact nothing less or more than a reality of living as Christians in a fallen and often hostile world.)

   - The purpose of trials

     (The surprising and encouraging perspective that the passage gives us is that trials, though painful, are under God's control. God uses trials to grow us to maturity.)

3. Responding to trials (1:5-8)

    - Ask the God who gives

        (We need wisdom to see trials God's way and to remain steadfast in the midst of trials.)

    - Trust the God who gives

        (God gives wisdom to all who ask, so let us ask freely and with confidence.)

    - Guard your heart

        (Trials expose the state of our hearts and provide the opportunity for us to be wholehearted in our relationship with God.)

4. A surprising example (1:9-11)

    - A surprising exaltation (1:9)
    - A surprising humiliation (1:10, 11)

        (Both wealth and poverty are a trial and should be seen not as the world sees them but in the light of God's wisdom.)

5. A surprising conclusion (1:12)

    - The way of blessing
    - The path to life

        (In God's good purpose, trials are the way of growth and the pathway to the crown of life. The way of steadfastness and perseverance is thus the way of blessing.)

Suggestions for teaching

Questions to help understand the passage

1. For whom are James' words in this passage intended?
2. What kinds of trials are in view in this passage?

3. What does the passage teach about
   - the purpose of trials?
   - the right response to trials?

4. What do we learn about God from this passage?

5. What imagery does James use in this passage? How do these images communicate James' key concerns?

6. What are the main verbs and key words/themes in the passage?

7. Divide the passage into subsections. What do you think the main idea of each section is?

8. In the light of your study of the passage, what do you think the main point of the passage is?

Questions to help apply the passage

1. In what way has James' teaching in this passage either confirmed or challenged your thinking about trials?

2. What do you find surprising in this passage?

3. What part of this passage do you find hardest to accept and put into practice?

4. In what way has this passage helped or encouraged you?

5. What have you learnt from this passage about the importance of guarding your heart?

6. In the light of this passage, what are some things to pray for yourself?

7. How could this passage help you to explain Christianity to someone who is not a Christian?

8. How can you use this passage to encourage a fellow believer?

3.
Facing Temptation
(James 1:13-18)

Introduction

In James 1:13-18 the focus shifts from the trials of life in a fallen world to the reality of temptation to sin. Trials may well provide an occasion for temptation and sin, but the real problem does not lie in our external circumstances but within our hearts. The double-mindedness that James warns against in 1:6-8 is nowhere more evident than in the struggle between our own sinful desires and the word of God. It is also evident in our propensity for blame-shifting when it comes to our failures and in our spiritual amnesia regarding God's good design for our lives. In keeping with his aim to encourage believers to persevere to the end in wholehearted devotion to the Lord, James does three things. First, he warns his readers about the danger of self-deception with regard to temptation and sin. Second, he reminds them of the danger of a life ruled by 'I want' rather than by 'God has said'. Third, he reminds them of the goodness of God and of His good purposes for His people.

Listening to the text

Context and structure

As noted earlier, the transition from 1:2-12 to 1:13-18 comes via the link words 'trial'/'temptation'. The passage can be subdivided into two parts – namely, 1:13-15 and 1:16-18. The first part begins with the imperative 'Let no one say' (1:13) and ends with another of James' proverbial sayings (1:15), which, with its focus on the downward spiral from sinful desire to death, stands in stark contrast to the path of steadfastness leading to life in 1:12. The key words in this section are 'tempt' (used five times) and 'desire' (used twice and linking 1:14 and 15). Thus, an important theme in this section is the dangerous relationship that exists between desire and temptation. As we shall see, the imagery of 1:14-15 is parallel to that of 1:18, thus unifying the two parts of the passage.

Although it is possible to see 1:16 as the conclusion of the preceding section, the vocative 'my beloved brothers' makes it more likely that the imperative 'Do not be deceived' relates to what follows in verses 17 and 18. The section ends with a statement reminding the readers of their spiritual privilege and responsibility (1:18). The imagery of this section, with its focus on 'the Father of lights' who gives good gifts – especially the gift of spiritual life by His 'word of truth' (1:17, 18) – stands in contrast to the imagery of 1:14-15, with its focus on evil desire that gives birth to sin and death. As noted above, this parallel but contrasting imagery unifies the passage as a whole.

Finally, we note that although there is a thematic link between 'the word of truth' (1:18) and 'the implanted word' (1:21), the vocative 'my beloved brothers' and the change of subject (from *facing temptation* to *hearing and doing the word*) make it clear that 1:19 begins a new section of the letter.

Working through the text

A strong corrective (1:13)

Having encouraged his readers to remain 'steadfast under trial' (1:12), James now issues a strong and personal corrective to his readers. Verse 13 begins with the exclamation 'no one' (literally, 'No one, when tempted, let him say ...'). James is about to assert something important and what he has to say applies to each of his readers personally and without exception. Furthermore, we note that James refers to *when* not *if* his readers face temptation. Temptation cannot be avoided. What must be avoided however is a response to temptation that seeks to shift responsibility away from the one being tempted and onto a scapegoat – in this case, God Himself.

Of course, the idea that anyone would blame God for temptation is a strange one, so much so that one might be tempted to translate the word 'tempted' in verse 13 as 'tested' throughout. But such a solution, while maintaining unity with 1:12, does not fit the context of 1:13-15, with its focus on evil desires, sin and death. Nor does it align with James' teaching in 1:2-12, where all testing is seen in a positive light as a God-given means of spiritual growth. One alternative is to translate the first occurrence of the word in verse 13 as 'tested' and the second as 'tempted', implying that someone who has fallen into sin in the midst of a time of testing responds by blaming God for allowing the test in the first place.[1] On reflection, this seems to be the best option, since it maintains the logical connection between 1:12 and 1:13 and does justice to the context of 1:13-15 as a whole. It also sketches the most likely scenario in which such blame-shifting might take place, especially if the one making such assertions is drifting toward being double-minded. This of course is the pattern our first parents adopted: being tested at the tree, succumbing to temptation and then blame-shifting – in Adam's case, blaming God with the words 'The woman whom you gave to be with me' (Gen. 3:12).

James' response to such wrong thinking is to affirm a fundamental truth about God. Not only is God *not* tempted with evil, He '*cannot be* tempted with evil' since 'he himself tempts no one' (1:13). The phrase 'he himself' is emphatic, underlining the fact that God will in no way and at no time ever tempt anyone. Wherever temptation comes from, it does not come from God.

An honest assessment (1:14)

In 1:14, James moves from a strong personal corrective to an honest assessment. The phrase 'But each person' is once again inclusive of all and provides a clear alternative to the erroneous view set out in 1:13. Elsewhere in the letter, James warns against the polluting effect of a world at enmity with God (1:27; 4:4) as well as the deceptive and destructive work of the evil one (3:15; 4:7). But in this passage the single focus is upon the deceptive power of our own sinful desires. James' use of the words 'lured' and 'enticed' (1:14) creates another of his powerful images, though with a

---

1. This is the view taken, inter alia, by McCartney (2009: 104 ff.), McKnight (2011: 115) and Moo (2000: 72).

sting in the tail; for we might naturally use these words for the deceptive pull of the world or the evil one – that is, something outside of ourselves. James will have none of that kind of blame-shifting. In the final analysis, a key part of wholeheartedness and steadfastness in the faith is to face honestly the reality and the deceptiveness of one's own sinful desires and heart. As we shall see, this will mean that heartfelt repentance will be an important part of the normal Christian life (1:21; cf. 4:8-10).

A clear warning (1:15)

The section ends with another of James' proverbial sayings. Using the image of conception, birth and growth, James outlines a deadly cycle: desire cohabiting with temptation to give birth to sin, finally resulting in death. It is a terrible picture, one that James paints in stark terms without any softer tones. There is no mention of forgiveness or salvation; this is not because James does not see these as possible – indeed, quite the opposite (see e.g. 1:21; 4:8-10 and especially 5:19-20). Rather, James' point in this passage is to issue a clear warning to his readers precisely so that they can resist the pull of their own sinful desires and the danger of being double-minded and instead give themselves to wholehearted devotion and obedience to the Lord.

An urgent appeal (1:16-18)

In 1:16, the strong corrective, honest assessment and clear warning of 1:13-15 give way to an urgent appeal. James addresses his 'beloved brothers' directly and urges them not to be deceived. The word translated 'be deceived' is used again by James in 5:19 to describe those who 'wander' from the truth. Given that 1:16 introduces what follows, the truth that James wants his readers not to be deceived about, and thus not to wander from, is the truth about God the Father and His goodness. James describes God as the source of 'every good gift and every perfect gift' (1:17). The emphasis here is on the generosity of God and on the goodness and complete suitability of what He gives. Like wisdom generously given to those who ask in faith (1:5), all of God's good gifts come 'down from above'.

Furthermore, James wants his readers to be clear that the God who gives these gifts is the 'Father of lights' (1:17), the Creator who is without a shadow of change and who is utterly faithful and reliable. It is precisely because of His trustworthiness that they can turn to Him in faith and with confidence, not only when facing trials but also when confronted by temptation. Indeed, there is more to it than that. For God the giver of good gifts is the Father of His people in a very particular way. In stark contrast to desire that leads to sin and brings forth death, God the Father is the one who 'brought us forth by the word of truth' (1:18), entirely of 'his own will' and thus for His definite purpose. God's good purpose for His children has already been described in 1:4; it is that they should be 'perfect and complete, lacking in nothing.' As we shall see, this good purpose will only be fulfilled at the 'coming of the Lord' (5:7). But its outworking begins at the moment of spiritual birth among those who have the great privilege of being the 'firstfruits' (1:18) of a new creation. It is precisely in the light of this great privilege that James wants his readers to hold firmly to the truth and to withstand the false thinking and desires that so easily deceive and tempt us.

From text to message

Few things are more discouraging to genuine believers than the ongoing struggle that we have with temptation and sin. In times of victory we are of course filled with assurance. But when we fall we are overcome with doubts and even at times despair. The honest assessment of our hearts that James calls for is important, but it can be hard to bear, especially when we remember what is at stake! At times like these it is important that James 1:13-18 does more than reveal the reality of our fallen state. It also reminds us of the Father's great gifts to us, in particular the gift of new birth by His word of truth, the gospel. In preaching and teaching this passage, then, we need to take care to do two things: First, we do need to remind our hearers of the reality of our sinfulness and thus to warn them not to flirt with temptation. But we also need to remind our hearers of the reality of new birth and that, as those who belong to God, it is not only possible but essential to stand against temptation in the power that God gives. If James' aim in this passage is to urge us to say 'No!' to temptation, then he also urges us to do so by saying 'Yes!' to God.

Getting the message clear: the theme

God does not tempt His people to sin but has given them new birth through the word of truth, the gospel, so that they will resist temptation and obey His word.

Getting the message clear: the aim

To encourage believers to resist temptation and sinful desires by recognising the reality of their fallen condition and God's good purpose in giving them new birth.

A way in

One way in to preaching this passage could be to talk about the struggle that every believer faces with temptation. Temptation comes from various sources, but the biggest struggles we face are probably with the temptations that come from within. Do such temptations in fact mean that we are not believers at all? James' teaching on this important subject points us in a different direction, one that, though hard to hear, in fact leads us to real hope because it leads us away from our own strength and to God's good gift.

Another way in could be to start not with our struggle with temptation but with God's gift of new birth. One could ask a question concerning an agreed truth; for example, 'Why has God given new birth to His people?' The Bible gives us a number of answers to that question, and today we want to look at one very important but often neglected answer – namely, the role that new birth plays in our struggle against temptation and sin.

Ideas for application

- Every person faces temptation from within, and this is true even after we become Christians.

- Temptation may lead to sin, but it is not in itself sin.

- Part of maturity in Christ is found in our fight against temptation.

- God can be fully trusted in the midst of our struggle against temptation.

- God's purpose in giving us new birth is so that we can say 'No!' to temptation and 'Yes!' to God's word.

Suggestions for preaching

Sermon

Undivided (Talk 3)

'Facing Temptation' (James 1:13-18)

1. Introduction

   - Temptation: the struggle we all face

   - Denial: the common self-deception

2. A strong corrective (1:13)

   - Let no one say!

     (As fallen human beings, we are quick to blame others for our faults. To do this is not only to contradict Scripture, but in fact to close the door on a true solution.)

3. An honest assessment (1:14)

   - Our fallen condition

     (Although temptation does come from the world and the devil, it very definitely and perhaps most commonly comes from within our own hearts. Facing this reality is an important step in dealing with temptation.)

4. A clear warning (1:15)

   - The pathway to death

     (The truth is that though temptation is not in fact sin, left unchecked it will inevitably lead to sin. And if we indulge ourselves in this way, our sins very easily become habitual, with deadly spiritual consequences if we don't take steps to stop the decline.)

5. An urgent appeal (1:16-18)

- Don't be deceived

  (Just as we are not to be deceived about temptation we are not to be deceived or to wander away from the truth about God's true character.)

- God the giver of good gifts

  (God's character is shown in His generosity and stead-fastness and in the goodness of the gifts He gives.)

- The greatest gift of all

  (God's gift of new birth by His word of truth is intended to empower us to resist temptation and pursue a godly life in accordance with His word. By this gift God enables us to be His wholehearted followers.)

Suggestions for teaching

Questions to help understand the passage

1. In what way does James 1:12 provide the context for what he says about temptation in 1:13-18? (Note: the word translated 'trial' in verse 12 and 'tempt' in verse 13 is the same word in the original.)

2. What are the imperatives in this passage?

3. What imagery does James use in this passage?

4. How does the imagery function to establish the main point of the passage?

5. What does the passage teach us about God?

6. In what way does James' teaching about God help to establish his main point?

7. What does this passage teach about new birth?

Questions to help apply the passage

1. In what way has James' teaching in this passage either confirmed or challenged your thinking about temptation?

2. What do you find surprising in this passage?

3. What part of this passage do you find hardest to accept and to put into practice?

4. In what way has this passage helped or encouraged you?

5. What have you learnt from this passage about the importance of saying 'No!' to temptation?

6. In what way has this passage encouraged you toward wholehearted obedience?

7. In the light of this passage, what are some things to pray for yourself?

8. How could this passage help you to explain Christianity to someone who is not a Christian?

9. How can you use this passage to encourage a fellow believer?

4.
The Word-Shaped Life
(James 1:19-25)

Introduction

In James 1:18, James describes his readers as the firstfruits of God's creatures, brought forth by 'the word of truth'. In 1:19-25 he turns his attention to the way of life that God expects of them. This way of life is the way of righteousness (1:20), of true freedom (1:25), and thus of blessedness (1:25). It is brought about by God's 'implanted word' at work in believers, a word that we are not to resist in stubborn rebellion – especially when it challenges our thinking or our conduct – but rather to receive with humility and put into practice day by day. Given the emphasis in this section is on the word, we can thus describe this way of life that God expects of His people as the 'word-shaped life'.

Listening to the text

Context and structure

James 1:19-25 begins with an urgent appeal from James to his 'beloved brothers'. This appeal is followed by a series of imperatives – six in total in the passage and all occurring in the opening verses (1:19-22). Two statements (1:20, 25) give the motivation behind these imperatives and focus attention on the purpose of God (1:20) accomplished by the implanted word (1:21). The repeated focus on 'the word' (1:21, 22, 23; 'law' in 1:25) and on both hearing (1:19, 22, 23, 25) and doing (1:22, 23, 25) the word, emphasises the importance of our response to God's implanted word in the accomplishment of God's purpose. The series of imperatives plus the image of the word as a mirror (1:23, 24) highlight both the logic and the urgency of this response.

Although it is possible to include 1:26-27 with 1:19-25, we have chosen to treat it as a section in its own right. We will give reasons for this decision in our discussion of the context and structure of 1:26-27 in the next chapter.

Working through the text

Receiving the word (1:19-21)

Having described his readers as those who have been brought forth by God's word of truth to be the firstfruits of His creatures (1:18), James now addresses them in characteristic terms as his 'beloved brothers' (1:19). Together they are part of the family of God and as such they are to think clearly about God's purposes for each of His people. James wants each believer to 'know' (1:19) that there is a righteousness of God that must be produced in the life of a believer (1:20). This is the first of three references to 'righteousness' in the letter (cf. 2:23 and 3:18). In 2:23 the context makes it clear that James is referring to righteousness as justification (see the discussion of 2:14-26). In 3:18 James speaks about righteousness in relation to 'good conduct' and works done in the 'meekness of wisdom' (3:13). The reference to meekness in 1:21 and the later emphasis on hearing and doing the word (1:22-25) suggest that in 1:19-21, James is talking about the righteous life that God desires in His people rather than justification.

For such righteousness or godliness to be produced, it is imperative that each believer receive the implanted word with meekness. The command to 'receive ... the implanted word' is curious since it mixes activity and passivity. How does one *receive* that which is *implanted?* As we look at what James says in this passage, we note that the first imperative is an exhortation to 'hear' rather than to 'speak' or become angry. In the context of 'the word', this hearing must refer to our being quick to hear the word and slow to speak against what it says or become angry when the word challenges our way of thinking or our behaviour. Such hearing rather than defensive gainsaying is what it means to receive the implanted word with meekness. But such hearing can only flow from a willingness to be changed by the word. Thus, James' command to his readers to receive the word 'with meekness' carries with it a call to 'put away all filthiness and rampant wickedness' (1:21) so that they will be able to receive the word in the right way.

The call to 'put away all filthiness and rampant wickedness' is striking and worthy of further consideration. The image is that of removing a soiled garment (cf. 2:2, where there is a man in, literally, 'filthy clothing'), but the striking point is that the filth is on the inside and thus a danger to the soul. 'Wickedness' is perhaps better translated 'evil' or 'malice', and this once again suggests an inner heart condition rather than specific deeds. Furthermore, the salvation spoken of in 1:21 is surely eschatological, a salvation that comes to the one who does not wander (5:20) but rather perseveres to the end (cf. 1:12; 1:25). James' key concern in this passage then is that his readers, having been brought forth by the word of truth, continue in a humble and repentant attitude of heart and mind toward that implanted word, putting aside everything that would tend to make them 'double-minded' and divided in soul.

Doing the word (1:22-25)

The call to 'receive with meekness the implanted word' (1:21) leads logically to the exhortation to 'be doers of the word' (1:22). Because God accomplishes His righteous purposes in the lives of His people through His word, this word must be heard in order to be received. But, as in the parable of the sower, this raises questions about kinds of hearers. James contrasts two in particular. On the one hand, there is the hearer who only hears but does not do the word. James characterises such a hearer in negative terms as self-deceived (1:22) and forgetful (1:24, 25). Seen in the light of James' analogy of a man looking into a mirror who does not act on what he sees but forgets what he looks like, this forgetfulness implies spiritual and moral folly. This is confirmed when one notes James' description of what this 'mirror of the word' actually is. For the word that is heard is no mere human wisdom (cf. 3:15) but God's perfect 'law of liberty' (1:25). To ignore the former is no great thing, but to ignore the latter is nothing short of disastrous.

For this reason James urges each of his readers to be the right kind of hearer – namely, a hearer who is not a hearer only (1:22) but a 'doer who acts' (1:25). Having looked into God's perfect, liberating law and thus seen themselves clearly as God does, such a hearer necessarily acts, putting into practice what the perfect law says. Nor is this a simple, one-off matter. For God's righteous purposes for His people, though they begin at the moment of new birth, are worked out over time. They will not be completed until the final day of eschatological salvation. Thus, James urges his readers to persevere in this practice of hearing and doing, reminding them that this alone is the pathway of and to blessing (1:25).

From text to message

One of the challenges of living in a world dominated by words is that words end up losing their power to change lives. Where words are many, talk is cheap, and the art of listening suffers. And of course, when such a world is not only word saturated but also pluralistic, relativistic and centred on the cult of self, it becomes increasingly difficult to present one particular message as *the* truth, a word that all people should hear, receive and obey. And yet that is precisely the task that Christians have been given. But before we are called to speak the word of truth to the world, we are called to be people of the word ourselves – people who are humble before the word, keen to hear the word and eager to put it into practice. It is for this reason that James 1:19-25 is such an important passage both to read and to preach. For the spirit of the world finds its way into the church. And the word-shaped life to which we are called does from time to time face a rival way of life, one that may seem more relevant to our culture and, in the short term at least, more spiritual. Indeed, nothing would please the enemy of our souls more than if we fell prey to the sin either of hearing the word of God as a mere academic exercise without it changing our lives, or of seeking that change by some other means, apart from or in addition to the word.

Getting the message clear: the theme

God's word is His perfect law, the means by which He brings true liberty and righteousness to His people, resulting in final salvation.

Because God's word is the means by which He works to save His people, God's people should hear and receive God's word with meekness and continue to put what it says into practice.

Getting the message clear: the aim

To remind God's people of the power and sufficiency of God's word and to urge and encourage them to persevere in hearing, receiving and doing God's word.

A way in

One way in to preaching this passage could be to highlight the nature of our culture as word saturated (think of social media) but also relativistic, pluralistic and self-centred. Such a culture is intolerant of absolutes and thus impatient with claims for the authority and sufficiency of Scripture. James 1:19-25 challenges that prevailing culture and urges us to treat God's word with the respect that it deserves, not sitting in judgment over it but rather submitting to it as a unique and powerful force to change our lives.

An alternative way in could be to warn against hypocrisy in our walk with Christ. Jesus certainly opposed all forms of hypocrisy, and the watching world uses the hypocrisy of people who claim to be Christian as a reason for rejecting the faith. James 1:19-25 challenges hypocrisy, reminding us that God expects us not only to hear but also to do His word. Indeed, when we look more closely, we see that this is a salvation issue and thus that it must be treated with the utmost seriousness.

Ideas for application

- The wisdom saying in 1:19 does not apply to speech and anger in general but to how we respond to God's word. We should be quick to hear it and slow to speak our own opinion, and we should never reject God's word even when it challenges us deeply.

- God's word is the means by which He changes us day by day.

- Repentance is not only a result of listening to God's word – it is the key requirement to truly being able to hear and receive God's word.

- Obedience to God's word is non-negotiable for God's people.

- Only God's word provides the path to true freedom and blessing.

Suggestions for preaching

Sermon

Undivided (Talk 4)

'The Word-Shaped Life' (James 1:19-25)

1. Introduction

   - Our world: a world full of words, unwilling to listen

   - Our challenge: to respond to God's word correctly

2. Receiving the word (1:19–21)

    - God's word – the means of righteousness and salvation

      (God implants His word within us when He regenerates us. And it is by this implanted word that God powerfully works within us to lead us along the path of righteousness to our final salvation. Acknowledging that God works by His word is essential for a right response to His word.)

    - Responding to God's word – our responsibility in the light of God's work in us

      (God's work in us by His word requires our work in response. The right response to God's work is repentance in the light of His word and a humble, receptive attitude toward God's word.)

3. Doing the word (1:22-25)

    - How not to hear!

      (Those who hear God's word but do not put it into practice fall prey to the folly of spiritual forgetfulness and end up self-deceived. As with all spiritual folly, this is not a healthy condition to be in, hence James' urgent appeal in 1:22.)

    - The right way to listen!

      (Rather than being hearers who forget, God's people are to cultivate the habit of putting the word that they hear into practice. God's word is designed to produce a righteous way of life for His people. That necessarily means that we are to live out what His word says.)

    - The path of freedom and blessing!

      (Although our sinful nature and the prevailing culture assure us that we know best and have the right to

choose our own path of freedom, obedience to God's word is the right path. God's word is the perfect law – trustworthy and reliable instruction for life. And God's word liberates us from our folly and sin, thus proving to be the means of true blessing in our lives.)

Suggestions for teaching

Questions to help understand the passage

1. Divide the passage into subsections. What do you think is the main theme of each section?

2. What are the main imperatives in this passage?

3. The exhortation 'be quick to hear, slow to speak, slow to anger' can easily be turned into general moral wisdom. What does this exhortation mean in the context of 1:19-25?

4. What does the phrase 'the righteousness that God requires' mean in the context of 1:19-25?

5. The call to 'receive with meekness the implanted word' sounds paradoxical. What does James mean when he urges his readers to do this?

6. How do the commands to 'put away' and 'receive' in 1:21 relate to each other?

7. What does James mean by 'salvation' and 'blessing' in this passage?

8. What does James mean when he describes God's word as 'the perfect law, the law of liberty' (1:25)?

Questions to help apply the passage

1. In what ways has this passage challenged you in your attitude to God's word?

2. What have you learnt from this passage about the value of God's word?

3. What does 1:21 teach us about repentance?

4. What do we learn from 1:22-25 about how to truly hear the word of God?

5. Our modern culture often construes the Bible's teaching as restrictive and thus oppressive. How would you counter this view from 1:22-25?

6. In what way has this passage encouraged you toward wholehearted obedience?

7 In the light of this passage, what are some things to pray for yourself?

8. How could this passage help you to explain Christianity to someone who is not a Christian?

9. How can you use this passage to encourage a fellow believer?

5.
True Religion
(James 1:26-27)

Introduction

There are doubtless many in our society for whom the word *religion* has negative connotations. Secularists and naturalists are outspoken about the irrelevance and, in more extreme cases, even the danger of religion. And of course there is the ugly phenomenon of 'empty religion': religion as external ritual with little or no thought of true relationship with God and no power for change in the life of those who follow it. Such hypocritical religion is all too prevalent in our world and is rightly spoken against because it is demeaning to God and to people.

In the light of such a perspective on *religion*, James' exposition of the nature of true religion is both striking and important. As we have already noted, James is deeply concerned about the state of the hearts of his readers. His appeal in 1:26-27 is thus not for religion per se but for a religion that is both 'pure and undefiled', a practical religion that is a true expression of wholehearted faith.

Listening to the text

Context and structure

The decision to treat 1:26-27 as a section in its own right is based upon a number of factors. First, note the introduction and repetition of the word 'religion' (1:26, 27), only used here in the letter. Second, although the act of visiting orphans and widows in their affliction (1:27) is undoubtedly an example of 'doing the word' (1:25), there is no explicit reference to 'the word' in 1:26,27. This is in marked contrast to 1:19-25 with its focus on 'the word'. Third, although one could argue for a logical connection between the 'law of liberty' (1:25) and a 'pure and undefiled' religion (1:27), the same is true for the connection between such religion as set out in 1:26-27 and the 'royal law' (2:8). Yet, 2:1-13 is clearly a separate unit (see below). Finally, although 1:26-27 clearly echoes some of the key themes of 1:2-25, it also anticipates what follows in 2:1ff. Thus, it seems best to treat 1:26-27 as a transitional paragraph connecting and bridging chapter 1 to the rest of the letter. As we shall see when discussing 1:26-27, the reference to remaining 'unstained from the world' ties in with the letter's overall emphasis on the importance of wholehearted perseverance toward maturity.

Working through the text

Worthless religion (1:26)

James begins his exposition of true religion by pointing out the folly and spiritual danger of a religion that, however sincerely or strictly adhered to, fails to make any practical difference in the life of the adherent. Although there are any number of areas that James could highlight to show this folly and self-deception, he chooses the example of the unbridled tongue (1:26), to which he will return in greater detail in 3:1-12. As we shall see in our discussion of 3:11-12, the choice of the unbridled tongue as an example is particularly apt because James' primary concern is not simply with conduct but also with the heart from which such conduct flows. An unbridled tongue reveals something about the heart of the person (cf. Matt. 12:33-37) and shows that heart to be deceived. James earlier urged his readers not to be deceived about temptation, sin and God's good gifts (1:16). And in 5:19 he expresses pastoral concern for the restoration of the believer who 'wanders from the truth' (literally, has been 'deceived' away from the truth). Although the word used in 1:26 is a different word, the semantic connection is clear and underlines James' concern that the so-called religious person with the unbridled tongue has a wandering heart, a heart that in fact has become polluted by the world (see 1:27 below). In sum then, such 'religion', far from being 'pure and undefiled' (1:27), is in fact 'worthless' (1:26) – that is, empty and of no value for salvation, just like the deedless faith of 2:14-17 (see the chapter on 2:14-26).

Religion: pure and undefiled (1:27)

In contrast to 'worthless' religion, James holds out the prospect of a religion that is 'pure and undefiled' (1:27). The point of reference for evaluating such religion is not oneself (cf. 1:26) but 'God, the Father,' who sees truly and thus evaluates accurately. 'Pure and undefiled' refers to that which God the Father considers to be true, holy and acceptable. For Jewish Christian readers this language

would in all likelihood have carried echoes of the way of
approach to God as set out in the Scriptures (e.g. Ps. 24:3)
and now fulfilled through Christ. But it would also have
stirred memories of the stinging prophetic rebuke against
religious ritual that was devoid of mercy and compassion
(e.g. Isa. 1:12-17). And here the reference to God as Father is
particularly striking, for the Scriptures make it crystal clear
that God is indeed 'Father of the fatherless and protector
of widows' (Ps. 68:5). Since this is so, then surely it is to be
expected that those whom the Father has brought forth by
the word of truth (1:18) will themselves 'visit [i.e. care for]
orphans and widows in their affliction' (1:27). Here again
James reminds his readers of the need to be not simply
hearers but doers of the word! We may thus say that true
religion must of necessity be practical religion.

If religion devoid of charity is repudiated as deceptive
and worthless, then so too is religion that is devoid of
holiness – or in James' language, religion that fails to
withstand the contaminating and defiling influence
of the world (1:27). This is the first of three instances
where James speaks of the 'world' in negative terms (cf.
4:4). As we shall see in 4:4, to choose friendship with the
world is in fact to put oneself at enmity with God and is
tantamount to spiritual adultery. But in 1:27 the choice
comes in terms of positive and persevering resistance to
the pressure that the world seeks to exert. And, as we
have already seen and will see again, there is no area in
which the world is more deceptive and defiling than when
it cloaks our pride and greed in the guise of religion. Such
worldly religion is indeed worthless! It is shaped by the
wisdom of the world rather than by the word and the
Spirit of God (cf. 3:13–4:10). It is devoid of repentance

(cf. 1:21; 4:8-10) and thus leaves the unholy fruits of our fallen nature and divided hearts unchallenged and unchanged. It is thus the 'worthless religion' of the double-minded person (cf. 1:8; 4:8), a religion of form but one devoid of power to accomplish God's righteous purposes for His people (cf. 1:4, 12).

From text to message

Given the duality of a society characterised both by secularism and superstition, the opportunity that James 1:26-27 provides to preach about true religion is a valuable one. In contrast to those who see religion as nothing more than rank hypocrisy and a means to exploit or control others, James' definition of true religion is striking indeed. Far from being a human social construct, true religion is one of God's good gifts, something to be measured against His standards and to be practised in sincere dependence upon Him. Far from being a means of exploiting others, true religion is a means of expressing our love for God the Father in our loving and compassionate treatment of those who are so often despised and neglected. And far from empty hypocrisy, true religion should be characterised by a deep moral integrity which says 'No' to the philosophy and moral standards of the world in order to say 'Yes' to godly wisdom and conduct in every area of life.

And, in contrast to those who see all religion as the same, something to be validated provided it is accompanied by sincerity of heart, James' distinction between deceptive and worthless religion and a religion that is pure and undefiled is of the utmost importance. All religions are not the same; all roads do not lead to God, for it is God, not our culture, who is the final adjudicator of our religion.

In religion, as in so much else, it is not truth *or* sincerity, but truth *and* sincerity that matters.

Getting the message clear: the theme

God, not human culture, is the arbiter of true religion.

True religion arises out of a relationship with God the Father. It is characterised by love expressed in acts of mercy and kindness and by holiness which is able to withstand the defiling influence of the world.

Getting the message clear: the aim

To encourage and challenge professing Christians to evaluate their own religion and to practise the religion that God the Father esteems and values.

A way in

Given the confusion within our society and even among believers about the word *religion*, one way in could be to look at the word *religion* and the different attitudes that people have toward it. Perhaps begin with the question 'What is true religion?' and point out that it is an important question, albeit a curious and – for some perhaps – even an inappropriate one. Some in our pluralistic culture may struggle with the word *true*. Others in our secular culture or within our particular Christian tradition, where we sometimes set religion and relationship with God as antitheses, may well find the word *religion* difficult to accept. James 1:26-27 provides us with a striking answer to our question – one that enables us to keep religion as an important word but also to fill it with true content.

An alternative way in could be to pick up the ever-present danger of hypocrisy. Of course, some people accuse Christians of being hypocrites because they fail to understand that true Christianity is about forgiveness and grace for sinners. But we do well to remember that if our religion lacks authenticity, and especially the power to do good and to be different from the world, it is hardly going to be attractive to the outsider. James warns us against hypocritical, powerless religion and offers an authentic alternative through the gospel.

Ideas for application

- Contrary to popular opinion, religion is not a personal matter but must be evaluated by objective standards.

- The only valid standards by which true religion can be measured are those which God the Father sets.

- True religion is certainly heart religion – religion that enables us to stand wholeheartedly for God in a world that seeks to draw us away from Him.

- True religion will always be practical – religion that finds expression in everyday life and in acts of love and compassion. These acts of love and compassion will be seen particularly in our care of those who are most vulnerable in society.

- True religion thus mirrors God's character and values in the life of those who adhere to it. True religion will thus always be evidenced in repentance and holiness.

- True religion will always be counter-cultural and will enable us to resist being governed by the philosophies and moral standards of the world.

Suggestions for preaching

Sermon

Undivided (Talk 5)

'True Religion' (James 1:26-27)

1. Introduction

   - What is true religion?

     - A curious, even inappropriate question?

       (Can we speak of true religion in a pluralistic world? Should we speak of religion at all in the light of the abuse of religion?)

     - An important question!

       (James clearly considers the subject of true religion to be important and we should take our lead from him and listen carefully to what he has to say.)

2. Worthless religion (1:26)

   - When sincerity and/or form are not enough.

     (Though many consider sincerity and zeal and/or correct form to be the measure of true religion, James warns against being deceived in our evaluation of our religion. Contrary to common opinion, there is in fact a religion that is totally worthless. Strikingly enough, such worthlessness is measured by the failure of our religion to change our hearts, as evidenced by our speech about and toward others. If our religion does not translate from words of praise to God into words of kindness and edification toward others, it is worse than useless!)

3. Religion: pure and undefiled (1:27)

- Practical religion

  (Religion that God values is religion that mirrors His attitude and behaviour toward those who are most vulnerable. True religion thus leads to the imitation of God.)

- Religion that transforms

  (Religion that is godly will inevitably arise from God's work in our hearts by His word and Spirit. Thus, it will enable us to withstand the pressure of the world rather than baptise the world's agenda into our religious practice and values.)

Suggestions for teaching

Questions to help understand the passage

1. What characterises worthless religion according to James?

2. Why is such religion dangerous for those who practise it?

3. What is the link in James 1:26-27 between the tongue and the heart?

4. By what standards should religion be measured? How is this different from the way the world thinks about religion?

5. Why does James single out the care of orphans and widows as a measure of true religion?

6. How are the words 'pure', 'undefiled' and 'unstained' connected in James' argument in 1:27?

7. What does James mean when he says that true religion involves remaining unstained by the world?

8. Note the reference to 'God, the Father' and 'the world' in 1:27. How do these terms stand in contrast to each other in this verse?

9. What do you think the main emphasis is of 1:26-27?

10. What do you think the main aim is in 1:26-27?

Questions to help apply the passage

1. In what way(s) has James 1:26-27 challenged your thinking about religion?

2. In the light of these verses, how would you evaluate your own religion?

3. What changes do you need to make in the light of these verses?

4. How could you use James 1:26-27 to answer the charge that religion is designed to exploit the needy and the vulnerable?

5. How could you use James 1:26-27 to answer the charge that all Christianity is hypocrisy?

6. How could you use James 1:26-27 to answer the claim that all religions are the same?

7. What is your prayer response to James 1:26-27?

6.

Seeing People God's Way
(James 2:1-13)

Introduction

'So whatever you wish that others would do to you, do also to them, for this is the Law and the Prophets' (Matt. 7:12). These familiar and challenging words from Jesus remind us that our treatment of others is a key aspect of Christian behaviour, one of the things that should mark us out as different from the world. In James 2:1-13, we are reminded that this 'golden rule' is as relevant for our Christian gathering as it is for our daily interaction with others.

The passage begins with a clear command to 'show no partiality' (2:1) in our attitude and actions toward others. Then, in typical James style, it illustrates this wide-ranging command by sketching a disturbing picture drawn from a Christian assembly (2:2-4). Once again, the focus is on economic disparity (cf. 1:9-11) and the challenge that this poses for the believers. In particular, James challenges his readers to see and to treat all people not by worldly standards but in the light of how God views and treats them. James' language is blunt and confrontational, though its overall aim is not simply to warn or rebuke but to persuade. By way of warning and rebuke, James reminds us that God, who is the only true and righteous judge, will not tolerate discrimination or favouritism, no matter how we may self-justify or rationalise our conduct. By way of persuasion, James reminds us that seeing and treating people God's way is the only logical and consistent response of those who have put their faith in Jesus the Lord of glory (2:1) and who themselves are debtors to His mercy (2:13).

Listening to the text

Context and structure

The exhortation to 'keep oneself unstained from the world' (1:27) leads logically to the command to avoid one common form of worldliness – namely, the tendency to show partiality toward the rich and influential. As is often the case in James, the direct address 'my brothers' (2:1) indicates the start of a new section. The negative command 'show no partiality' (2:1) is followed by two positive commands – namely, 'listen' (2:5) and 'so speak and so act' (2:12). These three imperatives, together with a string of rhetorical questions (2:4-7), drive the logic of the passage toward James' desired outcome: a way of speaking and acting in relation to the poor that is appropriate for those who understand God's gracious choice in giving the gift of faith (2:5), who bear the name of Christ (2:7) and who must therefore give an account before Him (2:12).

The noun 'partiality' (2:1) and the verb 'show partiality' (2:9) unite 2:1-7 and 2:8-13 into a single unit consisting of two subsections. The quotation of the royal law – 'You shall love your neighbour as yourself' (2:8) – denounces such partiality as 'sin' (2:9), adding further weight to the exhortation not to dishonour the poor but rather to show them love and respect. The theme of judgment (2:4) is continued in 2:12-13, which concludes the section with a typical, longer proverbial saying (2:13). Finally, it should be noted that, although 2:14-26 continues the theme both of faith and of deeds referenced in 2:1 and 2:12, the lack of any reference to partiality or judgment in 2:14-26 suggests that this is a distinct unit and thus worth considering on its own terms.

Working through the text

The sin of partiality (2:1-7)

'But you have dishonoured the poor man' (2:6)! This stinging rebuke reminds us that James 2:1-7 was no mere theoretical debate for James or for his readers. James wants his 'beloved brothers' (2:5) to 'listen' to his word, to be persuaded by his argument and to act in a way that is appropriate for those who 'hold the faith in our Lord Jesus Christ' (2:1). In context, this is a reference to the personal faith commitment of each believer – that is, faith *in* Jesus Christ who is 'the Lord' not only of believers but 'of glory' (2:1). Given who their Lord is, James urges his believing readers to be no respecters of persons and 'show no partiality' (2:1) as they live out their faith in Christ.

The partiality against which James speaks in general terms is now given particular illustration. The scene is the Christian assembly, gathered either to settle a dispute or, more likely, for the hearing and teaching of the word (cf. 1:22-25; 3:1-5). Enter two people from very different socio-economic situations who are then treated not as they ought to be, with equal respect and dignity, but in a worldly fashion. The wealthy person is given special attention and a prominent seat, while the poor person is treated with careless disdain: "'You stand over there", or, "Sit down at my feet'" (2:3). James does not specify whether either the wealthy person or the poor person is a believer, since his point is not their faith status but the inconsistency of the believers' conduct given their faith profession. James exposes this inconsistency of profession and practice with a string of rhetorical questions centred around his stinging rebuke in 2:6 and designed to show such partiality for the folly and sin that it is.

First, such conduct casts the believers in the role of judges – which they are not (cf. 4:12) – and in fact judges with 'evil thoughts' (2:4). The essence of the Lord's righteous judgments is that they are fair and just without regard for persons. How can those who claim to follow this Lord then show partiality? Second, we can look at God's treatment of the poor: far from disdaining them, God is pleased to bestow His gift of faith in the Lord Jesus on those who are poor by the world's standards and to give them an inheritance in His promised kingdom, the home of those who love Him (2:5). How can those who call God 'Father' and all believers 'brothers' treat those whom God has chosen with disdain? Third (and in terms of their inconsistency most telling), the believers are in fact aligning themselves with the standard of a world that is in fact hostile to their faith and blasphemes their Lord. Thinking for a moment would remind them that it is often the rich who stand opposed to the Christian faith and to the Christian's Lord (2:6-7). To show partiality toward the rich is thus to bring dishonour to the name of Christ.

And rather than gaining respect among the wealthy and powerful of society by being different from the world (cf. 1:27), such conduct only serves to portray the church as 'worldly'. Hardly an attractive quality in a community that should be ruled by God's word and standards. For as James has made clear in 1:9-10, in God's economy rich and poor stand on level ground and should be treated with equal dignity and respect.

The better way (2:8-13)

Having outlined a pattern of behaviour that is not only inconsistent with authentic faith but also offensive to the Lord, James now sets out a better way of speaking and acting for his readers (2:12). They are not to speak and act toward others as those who sit in the seat of judges but rather as those who will themselves be 'judged under the law of liberty' (2:12). James is here referring to 'the royal law according to the Scripture' (2:8), encapsulated in the command from Leviticus 19:18. The context of this command in Leviticus 19 is striking. There are warnings against exploiting the poor and the marginalised (19:9-10); stealing and bearing false witness (19:11-12); oppressing those who are in need or at risk (19:13-14); slandering, hating and taking vengeance (19:16-18); and, most important in terms of James 2:1-13, against showing partiality in court toward the rich, at the expense of the poor (19:15). In referencing Leviticus 19:18 as part of his argument, James thus reminds his predominantly Jewish Christian readers that the royal law in Scripture (given by God and sanctioned by Jesus) is fully binding on them not only in their legal assembly but whenever they gather.

Furthermore, the royal command to love one's neighbour as oneself is all-encompassing (James 2:8-11). It does not permit one to pick and choose areas of obedience or to play one part of the law off against another. In James' words, whoever 'fails in one point has become accountable for all of it' (2:10). Showing partiality is as much a transgression of Jesus' royal law as adultery or murder are and as such is a serious sin (2:9). Nor can partiality toward the wealthy be justified as loving the wealthy neighbour as oneself (note 'If you really fulfil' in 2:8), for it inevitably means a lack of love for the one facing discrimination. And such transgression rightly invokes divine judgment, where everyone should by rights be given exactly what they deserve without any respect of persons.

But, as James' readers would have known all too well, no one could in fact stand if judgment is devoid of mercy. This once again enables James to show the failure of his readers to be consistent in their thinking and action. They would want to experience mercy not judgment at the hands of God, and yet by discriminating against the poor and weak they fail to show mercy. If mercy is indeed to triumph over judgment for them (2:13), they should allow mercy to triumph over their own worldly discriminatory judgment of others. The way for this to happen is for them to treat each person in a way that is consistent with the mercy given by and received from the Lord who shows mercy.

From text to message

Experience shows that the sin of partiality remains one of humanity's besetting sins. Sadly, in this regard Christians are not exempt. Discrimination based on race, or gender, or socio-economic status is the bitter experience of many in our world and some in the church.

James 2:1-13 provides clear gospel-based teaching against the sin of partiality among Christians. It does not of course address the question of equality and role and therefore must not be used as a basis for discounting distinction of role in the name of non-discrimination. But it does identify partiality as a sin worthy of judgment and unworthy of those who follow Jesus. And it does remind us that how we treat others matters to God and should matter to us. Even in this sense alone it is a passage of enormous relevance and importance in our own day.

Getting the message clear: the theme

Partiality is a sin characteristic of the world but inconsistent with profession of faith in Jesus.

Partiality is a sin that will be judged by God and therefore a sin of which every Christian should repent.

Getting the message clear: the aim

To identify the sin of partiality for what it is and to root it out among those who profess faith in Jesus Christ.

A way in

Given the prevalence of partiality and unfair discrimination in our world, one way in could be to remind people of the problem and how unjust it is, especially when we are on the receiving end of such attitudes or behaviour. One could also highlight the failure and indeed inability of our modern culture to deal meaningfully with something that most people would in fact identify as wrong, even though they may not label it as sin. In contrast to this, James identifies the sin of partiality for what it is – an ugly example of worldly, double-mindedness among believers. But he also provides a solution by showing how faith in Jesus Christ, properly applied to life, enables one to change behaviour in this regard.

Ideas for application

- The sin of partiality is something that comes naturally to us as people. But as Christians who are called to remain unstained by the world, it is a sin that we must resist.

- Meaningful personal change requires clear understanding of truth about the area in which we want to change. James' strong rebuke of partiality is designed to bring the light of God's truth to this important area of life.

- Sin needs to be seen for what it is and plainly rebuked. Generalities and euphemisms will not bring about true change. James' case study of partiality is a clear example of this.

- The reality of divine judgment is a powerful incentive for change, even among Christians.

- Judgment and mercy should always be kept together in our preaching and teaching.

Suggestions for preaching

Sermon

Undivided (Talk 6)

'Seeing People God's Way' (James 2:1-13)

1. Introduction

- The problem of partiality

    ○ A common problem

    (Even though many in our society would not use the word 'sin' to describe partiality and unfair discrimination, it is recognised as something hurtful and 'wrong'.)

    ○ A stubborn problem

    (Notwithstanding the world's opposition to partiality and unfair discrimination, the problem persists, with little or no lasting remedy available from our unaided human wisdom.)

2. The sin of partiality (2:1-7)

- A clear command – show no partiality!

    (The clear command with which 2:1 begins makes it clear that James, speaking for the Lord, opposes all partiality, especially on the part of those who have faith in Christ.)

- A logical command – consider this!

    (James sketches a scenario in which partiality is practised, using the issue of wealth and poverty. He then shows by a variety of rhetorical questions how inconsistent and illogical such partiality toward the rich and powerful is for believers in Jesus.)

- A strong rebuke – but you have shown partiality!

    (Christians are not immune from the sin of partiality and are in fact guilty of it from time to time. It was so among James' readers and it may be so among us. Such sin must be rebuked in the strongest possible terms.)

3. The better way (2:8-13)

- God's royal law of love condemns the sin of partiality.

  ○ Partiality is the opposite of love.

    (Because partiality involves treating people differently based on standards set by this world, it is in fact harmful to all – those shown favour and those discriminated against. In this sense it is the opposite of love, which has the good of all in view.)

  ○ Partiality makes a mockery of God's law.

    (The sin of partiality encourages us to play fast and loose with God's standards, holding some as binding but others as discretionary. In the end we become the arbiters of right and wrong.)

  ○ Partiality will be judged.

    (When we practise the sin of partiality, we position ourselves as judges, and we fail to show mercy to those against whom we discriminate. Such conduct will be judged without mercy. And since mercy is what we need to survive judgment, we do well to practise mercy by repenting of all partiality in our dealings with others.)

Suggestions for teaching

Questions to help understand the passage

1. To whom is James directing his command prohibiting partiality?

2. In what way does the fact that Jesus is the Lord of glory underline the fact that partiality in our treatment of others is a sin?

3. What logic does James apply in this passage to show that the sin of partiality is contrary to how Christians ought to treat others?

4. What are the main commands in this passage?

5. How does James use Leviticus 19 to establish his argument against the sin of partiality?

6. What does James mean by the phrases 'royal law' and 'law of liberty'?

7. What role do the themes of judgment and mercy play in James' argument?

8. What do you think is the main emphasis of James 2:1-13?

9. What do you think is the main aim of James 2:1-13?

Questions to help apply the passage

1. How relevant do you think James' strong words against partiality are for your context?

2. Think of times when you have been unfairly treated. How did that make you feel?

3. In what ways are James' indictments against the wealthy and the powerful in this passage still relevant today?

4. How would James' words apply in a context where partiality is shown toward the poor and against the wealthy?

5. In what way does God's law in Leviticus 19 apply to us as Christians? How does James apply this law in the light of the gospel?

6. How would you use this passage to commend Christianity to someone who is not a believer?

7. In what way has James' teaching in this passage surprised, rebuked or encouraged you?

8. What is your prayer response to James 2:1-13?

7.
Faith That Saves
(James 2:14-26)

Introduction

Throughout his letter James' primary concern for his readers is that they remain wholehearted in their commitment to the Lord and steadfast in their walk with Him. For this reason the letter contains instructions, exhortations and earnest warnings.

In 1:26-27, James contrasts 'worthless' religion with religion that is 'pure and undefiled before God' so that his readers will not deceive their hearts (1:26). In James 2:14-26, James contrasts a faith that is 'dead' (2:17, 26) and thus 'useless' (2:20) with a faith that is able to save (2:14). Once again James' goal is to encourage his readers toward wholehearted perseverance in saving faith by giving a clear warning against the counterfeit, no matter how earnestly or sincerely held. Strikingly, as in 1:22-27, the difference is seen not in orthodox profession but in practical life. For James, as for the scriptural and dominical teaching that underlies his letter, saving faith is not 'lip service' faith but rather a faith that finds expression in works; a demonstrable, practical, and effective faith.

Of course, for those of us who read this letter as part of the New Testament today, the temptation is to read James' teaching about faith and works, especially his strong statement in 2:24, in the light of Paul's teaching on justification by faith alone. But to do this is to allow our theological framework to shape our reading of the text rather than let the text speak in its own terms. James' letter does contain important teaching on the theme of righteousness and justification, not least in 2:14-26. But both the early date and the assumed historical context of the letter make it unlikely, in my opinion, that James was in fact writing to counter a particular misunderstanding of Paul's teaching on justification among his readers. In context, it seems more likely that James, like the prophets of old and in service of his Lord, was writing to warn against the spiritual danger of an empty profession of faith which though orthodox in content, proved to be fruitless and thus spurious in reality. Such a 'faith' was indeed a far cry from that of Abraham and Rahab. As we shall see, both of them were indeed justified by faith in the sight of God. In affirming this, James is in full agreement with Paul. James' concern is to highlight the exact nature of saving faith by drawing attention to the fact that in each case, justifying faith is, of necessity, evidenced in works.

Listening to the text

Context and structure

As we noted in our discussion of the structure of the letter, most writers agree that James 2:14-26 is a self-contained unit. This view is supported by the presence of the two rhetorical questions and the typical form of address ('my brothers') with which the section begins (2:14) as well as the characteristic short, pithy saying with which it ends (2:26). Furthermore, we note the threefold affirmation of the worthless nature of faith without works: 'faith by itself, if it does not have works, is *dead*' (2:17); 'faith apart from works is *useless*' (2:20); 'faith apart from works is *dead*' (2:26). As we shall see, this dead faith is useless precisely because it is unable to save, the point made in the second rhetorical question in 2:14.

Although the illustration in 2:15-16 is once again drawn from the category of wealth and poverty (a favourite category of James), the emphasis of the text is in fact not on generosity but on the true nature of saving faith. The words 'faith' (eleven times) and 'works' (twelve times) dominate the passage, but in each case the focus is not on works, essential though they are, but on faith. It is works that 'complete' faith (2:22), not the other way around. Even James' response to the imaginary interlocutor of 2:18 makes it clear that the focus is neither on 'faith' *or* 'works', nor on 'faith' *and* 'works', but on 'faith' demonstrated *by* 'works.' The emphasis of the passage is thus on the true nature of saving faith.

When it comes to the literary context of 2:14-26, careful thought is required. Both 2:12-13 and 3:1 speak about the reality of judgment. In 2:12-13, judgment is to be under the 'law of liberty' and a reminder is given that, though mercy triumphs over judgment, those who refuse to show mercy will not receive mercy. This is a reminder that those who pass safely through judgment will have demonstrated proof in life of their commitment to the royal law of liberty by which they are to be judged. Certain of future mercy, those whose religion is true (1:26, 27) will show mercy.

Another way of making this point, especially given James' earlier concern that his readers be doers as well as hearers of the word (1:22), is to speak about saving faith – that is, faith that will truly justify and lead one safely through judgment – as a faith finds expression in works. This is precisely the theme of 2:14-26. Furthermore, the logical and thematic connection between 2:14-26 and 2:8-13 is seen by the fact that the example of a working and thus saving faith that James chooses is precisely a work of mercy.

Working through the text

Searching questions (2:14-17)

Two searching questions, each rhetorical and each expecting a negative answer, begin James' exposé of the vain and useless faith of the deedless professor. James envisions a person who claims to have faith but who in reality 'does not have works' (2:14). Concerning such a person, two questions must be asked – namely, what good is the claim? And can such faith save? The answer to the second question provides the answer to the first. A workless faith cannot save anyone, and therefore claiming such a faith as able to save is a profitless act. No good at all comes from such a claim – in fact, quite the contrary.

In order to underline the counterclaim that he has made, James, in typical fashion, introduces a practical example. Enter someone in need of practical mercy: a meal to see them through the day and a piece of clothing to keep out the winter chill (2:15). Now imagine someone within the community who is able to give practical help but who responds with a devout prayer that the needy person may know the peace of God and 'be warmed and filled' (2:16). Such a person may well claim to be exercising true faith in the one God who answers prayer and is able to provide for those in need. But in reality his failure to act does no good for the person in need, nor does it do any good for him (2:16). Indeed, he misleads or deceives his own heart as to the worthless nature of his religion (1:26) and the emptiness of his claim to true faith. It is at this point that James clinches his argument with the first of three assertions about deedless faith: 'faith by itself, if it does not have works, is dead' (2:17). For James, saving faith is a faith that evidences itself as a living faith, a faith expressed not simply in prayer but in acts of mercy as the need arises. Not to act in such circumstances is not only to lack works but in fact to lack true saving faith!

A foolish objection (2:18-25)

Aside from the conundrum posed by the words of the speaker in 2:18, James' main point in this passage is quite clear. Mere profession of faith, no matter how orthodox, proves nothing. One may indeed affirm the unity of God, even in terms which echo the *Shema* ('God is one' in 2:19), but such profession by itself does not demonstrate saving faith. Indeed, even demons affirm such truth – but shudder at the prospect of impending judgment (2:19). And in stark contrast, Abraham, who according to Scripture was counted righteous through faith (2:23; cf. Gen. 15:6), demonstrated the reality of his faith by his works, so much so that James can describe his offering up of Isaac as the active expression and completion (literally,

'perfection') of his faith (2:22). Thus, in James' terms, the
works described in Genesis 22 proved to be the fulfilment
of the faith described in Genesis 15:6 (2:23). Abraham
was thus characterised not by 'faith' *and* 'works', nor 'faith'
apart from 'works', but by 'faith' *demonstrated through*
'works' (2:18). In the final analysis, it was Abraham's action
not his profession that proved the justifying and thus the
saving nature of his faith.

Nor was this pattern (of authentic saving faith
demonstrated through works) true only of the great giants
of the faith such as Abraham. The exact same pattern
was found in the case of Rahab the prostitute whose
action in hiding and protecting the messengers was what
demonstrated the justifying and saving nature of her faith
(2:25; cf. Joshua 2). Thus, to return to the conundrum
in 2:18, any objection that sees both faith and works as
necessary but separable (as in, 'You have faith and [not *but*]
I have works') is essentially foolish (2:20) because it has
not understood the true and active nature of saving faith.
It is to this that James returns in a concluding statement.

The conclusion of the matter (2:26)

Having sought to establish the true nature of saving faith
and its counterfeit by example and from Scripture, James
ends with a striking metaphor to summarise and reinforce
the key point made in 2:17. Likening the relationship
between faith and works to the vital relationship between
body and spirit, James asserts once more that 'faith apart
from works is dead' (2:26). The metaphor deserves careful
consideration, for it does not say what one might have
expected – namely, that works without faith are dead.
This is of course true, but it is not the point that James

is making. His concern is not with dead *works* but with dead *faith*.

Consider the human body, says James. Apart from its animus or spirit (the breath of life, as it is called in Genesis 2:7), the body is essentially just a corpse. But with the life-giving spirit, the body is far more than a body – it is in fact a living person. So it is with saving faith. For at the very heart of saving faith we find not dormancy or inactivity but true life evidenced in works. Put differently, works lie at the very heart of saving faith.

This is saying more than that works are evidence of faith. This is true, of course, and central to James' argument. But it is only true because of the essential nature of saving faith. Because works lie at the very heart of saving faith, saving faith will always find expression in works. This is why an absence of works, whatever form they may take, is clear evidence that, despite claims to the contrary, such 'faith' is in the end not saving faith at all but rather a tragic delusion.

From text to message

Given our earlier comments about the importance of preaching the text rather than one's own theological framework, the key challenge in preaching James 2:14-26 is to ensure that it is indeed James' point which is both preached and applied. Doubtless, all of us know people who think that their own good works are a substitute for true faith in Jesus. But that is not who James has in view in this passage. His concern is with lip-service faith, and, truth be told, there is more spiritual danger from the latter than there is from the former. It is easier to call upon people to repent of dead works than of dead faith, especially if they are sincere.

Of course, in preaching this passage and insisting with James that true saving faith must be seen in our works, it is important to keep in mind that there will be some within the congregation who have an oversensitive conscience. For such hearers it is important to keep underlining that James is in fact still speaking about salvation by faith in the Lord Jesus, not some other kind of salvation. Though works matter as evidence of faith, they are not the basis of our salvation. At this point theological framework actually helps us not to push James' point too far with the result that we end up losing it all together.

Getting the message clear: the theme

Because works lie at the heart of saving faith, saving faith will never be apart from works.

Faith that truly justifies and saves will be evidenced by works.

Getting the message clear: the aim

To challenge those whose faith is merely lip-service to in fact exercise true saving faith in Christ.

To encourage those whose faith, while weak, is nevertheless active that they do indeed have true saving faith.

A way in

One way in could be via the saying 'Talk is cheap'. We all have experience of that in life, but sadly it is also true when it comes to claims to faith. More often than we would like to admit, we come across people who say all the right things but whose daily walk with the Lord is severely lacking. This not only confuses or discourages us, it also brings the gospel of the Lord Jesus into disrepute, opening the church up to the charge of hypocrisy. Of course, here as elsewhere, we are not called to judge others but to encourage them to judge themselves in the light of what God's word actually says. And in this regard James 2:14-26, with its identikit of true and living faith rather than dead and useless faith, is of great value.

Another way in could be in terms of the danger of self-deception. Not every claim to faith is valid and we do well to examine ourselves to ensure that the faith we lay claim to is indeed faith that saves. This passage helps us to do such an evaluation by providing us with an objective, practical measure to use.

Ideas for application

- We are not saved by orthodox doctrine but by true faith in the Lord Jesus.

- True faith in Jesus will always express itself in good works.

- As believers in the Lord Jesus we are expected to put our faith into practice.

- The works that flow out of true faith will always be consistent with what the gospel requires of us. Scripture remains the final judge of what is in fact a good work.

- No action that contradicts the plain teaching of Scripture should be considered a good work arising from true faith, even if it is labelled as such by our contemporary church culture.

- While true faith is always evidenced by good works, acts of mercy and kindness are not of themselves evidence of true faith.

■ In the final analysis, salvation is not by works
  (however good) but by faith in Jesus.

Suggestions for preaching

Sermon

Undivided (Talk 7)

'Faith That Saves' (James 2:14-26)

1. Introduction

   • 'Talk is cheap'
     (*All of us are angered or disappointed when people
     promise us things and then fail to deliver what they have
     promised. Talk is cheap, we say! The same is of course
     true when people make great boasts about themselves but
     then end up being a far cry from what they claim to be.*)

   • Lip service religion
     (*While false promises or empty boasting are frustrating
     and annoying in general, false promises or empty claims
     to faith among professing Christians are a serious matter.
     Not only do such things bring the gospel into disrepute,
     but they can also mislead people about the true state of
     their relationship with the Lord. It is for this reason that
     what James has to say in 2:14-26 is so important.*)

2. Searching questions (2:14-17)

   • What good is it?
     (*James prompts us to consider the nature of true saving
     faith as he asks two searching questions about the nature
     of faith. His aim is to bring us to the point where we can
     see for ourselves that faith without works is of no spiritual
     profit since it cannot save us.*)

- First refrain

  (In 2:17, James states his clear conviction about true faith for the first time. In so doing, he exposes the futile nature of faith apart from works, calling it dead faith.)

3. A foolish objection (2:18-25)

   - Empty talk

     (Lip service faith, no matter how orthodox in doctrine, is simply useless; worse than that, it is in fact diabolical. The demons have orthodox beliefs about God but are strangers to saving faith – to their own destruction. Mere profession of faith, however sincere, does not save anyone. And yet, tragically, such mere profession of faith is evident even in the best of churches. We ought to examine ourselves in the light of James' warning.)

   - Learning from Scripture

     (Both Abraham and Rahab, though coming from very different backgrounds and having a vastly different spiritual pedigree, teach the same important point. Faith and works are not two complementary virtues, both of which are needed for salvation. Salvation is by faith, but the faith that saves is of necessity a faith that shows itself in works. For this reason the act of separating works from faith is not merely foolish; it is spiritually dangerous.)

4. The conclusion of the matter (2:26)

   - A striking metaphor

     (Works are to faith, what the life force, or spirit, is to the body. Here again we see that James is not talking about dead works but dead faith.)

- Last refrain – key point

  (Faith that is devoid of works is dead. Such faith, being dead, cannot save no matter how sincere the claim of those who cling to it.)

Suggestions for teaching

Questions to help understand the passage

1. What key words or phrases are repeated in this passage?

2. James describes two kinds of faith in this passage. What does he say about each?

3. How does James use questions and statements to argue his point?

4. What role do the scriptural examples of Abraham and Rahab play in the establishment of James' point?

5. In 2:26 James uses a metaphor to describe faith. What is striking or surprising about what James says?

6. What is the main point that James is making in the passage?

Questions to help apply the passage

1. How do you think James' warning against dead and useless faith applies today?

2. How would you use James' argument in this passage to engage with the claim that Christians are 'so heavenly minded that they are of no earthly good'?

3. In what ways could James' teaching about faith and works be misunderstood? How would you correct these misunderstandings?

4. How would you use this passage to commend Christianity to someone who is not a believer?

5. In what way has James' teaching in this passage surprised, rebuked or encouraged you?

6. What is your prayer response to James 2:14-26?

8.

Words! Words! Words!

(James 3:1-12)

Introduction

'Sticks and stones may break my bones, but words can never harm me.' Like so many one-liners, this playground ditty, while it sounds clever, is completely inadequate for real life. The sad reality is that words can in fact cause great harm and lasting damage. Verbal abuse is a real and growing problem not only in the home but at school and at work. Gossip destroys reputations and can end someone's career, even if it is later shown to be false. And then there is the growing problem of 'fake news'. We live in a world of words and in this world, words matter. They are a powerful force for good and a terrible force for harm.

James 3:1-12 is all about words and the importance of all believers using words in the right way, but the passage speaks especially to those whose responsibility it is to teach others. Words are meant to instruct and so should be carefully weighed. Above all, those who claim the right to teach others, whether formally or informally, should remember that we will all give an account for our words

(3:1-5). And of course, in language that echoes Jesus'
teaching, words are a window on the human heart. What
comes out of our mouths not only has great effect on
others, but it shows us up for who we are. For this reason
all believers in Jesus, but especially teachers, should weigh
their words.

Listening to the text

Context and structure

Along with acts of mercy to those in need, there are no
works of faith more important to James than the ways that
believers speak to and about one another. In 1:26, James
speaks about the unbridled tongue as a clear indicator of a
religion that is worthless and a heart that has been defiled
by the world. In 2:12 James warns his readers to 'so *speak*
and so act as those who are to be judged under the law of
liberty.' It is thus not surprising that James returns to the
subject of the tongue directly after establishing that saving
faith is a faith that shows itself in works.

Once again the direct address 'my brothers' followed
by an imperative indicates the start of a new section. The
community at large is addressed, but the prohibition in 3:1
has a specific group in view – namely, would-be teachers.
In 3:2-12, James gives the reason for the prohibition, first
by means of a statement (3:2) and then through a series
of four striking analogies in support of the statement
(3:3-8). The repeated direct address 'my brothers' (3:10)
and the use of rhetorical questions (3:11-12) strengthen
the wisdom theme introduced by the analogies of 3:3-8
and thus provide a link to the discussion of two kinds of
wisdom in 3:13-18.

If, as a number of writers suggest, the focus in 3:13-18 is still on would-be teachers, then one may be tempted to treat 3:1-18 as a single unit. However, there are several good reasons for dealing with 3:13-18 as a separate, albeit closely connected section. First, there is James' propensity for the use of link words or ideas to transition from section to section; in this case the link is 'wisdom'. Second, we note the absence of any reference to the tongue or speech, which was so dominant a theme in 3:1-12. Third, we note the return to the idea of 'works' and 'good conduct' (3:13) as the demonstration of true wisdom in contrast to that which is false (cf. 2:14-26). Finally, we note the use of a short aphorism in 3:18 to end the unit in typical James style.

Working through the text

A reasoned prohibition (3:1-2)

The passage begins with a strong, though personal, warning from James to the whole community. Addressing them once again as 'brothers', James reminds his readers of something that they already know, something which should dissuade them from too easily stepping into the role of a teacher of others. What they know is that those 'who teach will be judged with greater strictness' (3:1), not only by their fellows but more particularly by the Lord. Some commentators take this to imply negative judgment or condemnation, but it seems more likely that James is making a general point: we are all accountable for what we say and all the more so if we presume the right to teach others. For this reason alone, 'not many … should become teachers' (3:1).

But, as if this high level of accountability for those who teach is not enough, James adds a further reason why not

many 'should become teachers'. The reason is found in
the reality of our human fallenness as evidenced in the
fact that everyone, including James, stumbles 'in many
ways' and, in this context, especially in 'what he says' (3:2).
Only the 'perfect man' (3:2) never stumbles in what he
says, ensuring that every word is completely aligned with
the 'perfect law' (1:25). Such a person has full control of
himself in every way just as a bridle and bit can be used by a
master horseman to fully control a horse (3:3). And indeed,
according to 1:19, such a person would be slow to speak
rather than presumptuous to teach. Such 'perfection' is, as
we saw in 1:4, the goal of God's wise and good work in His
people. But it remains an unfinished task this side of the
'coming of the Lord' (see 5:7). And thus, although James
does not prohibit all teaching of others (indeed quite the
contrary), he is adamant that '*not many* ... should become
teachers'.

Four striking analogies (3:3-8)

Having stated his reasoned prohibition in 3:1-2, James
now gives four striking analogies, each one designed to
show the danger of the tongue and thus to reinforce the
prohibition against many becoming teachers.

The first two analogies (the bit guiding the horse and
the rudder turning the ship in 3:3, 4) have a common
point. In each something small controls something
disproportionately large. The point of the analogy is then
given in a clear statement: 'the tongue is a small member,
yet it boasts of great things' (3:5). It is not immediately
clear from the passage exactly what these boasts are. What
is however clear is that notwithstanding the positive use of
'boast' in 1:9, James' other uses of the word are not positive

at all. Thus, in 3:14 boasting is a sign of selfish ambition and betrayal of the truth, while in 4:16 it is an expression of arrogance and is specifically defined as evil. Such boasting is thus more aligned with double-mindedness than with humble and wholehearted trust in the Lord. This propensity of the tongue to give vent to arrogance and selfish ambition among those whose hearts are divided and lack the humility that accompanies true wisdom (cf. 3:13) is precisely why not many should rush to become teachers.

The third analogy (a great forest fire started by a tiny spark in 3:5b) once again draws on the size element present in the first two. But whereas the first two analogies are positive in themselves, the analogy of a raging forest fire underlines the destructive nature of words. This is the point that James makes in his explanation of the analogy. The tongue, like the spark, may be a small member of the body, but its destructive power is immense. This is certainly true in terms of how words can destroy others, which I take it is what James has in mind when he describes the tongue as a 'world of unrighteousness' (3:6). Such a 'world of unrighteousness' is the polar opposite of God's righteousness (1:20) or the 'harvest of righteousness' that is 'sown in peace by those who make peace' (3:18). In all likelihood it refers to the harsh and destructive speech used either out of jealousy of those who have more (cf. 4:2, 11) or in disdain or, even worse, in abuse of those of lesser socio-economic standing (cf. 2:7; 5:6). Such speech is of course a window into a divided heart which has been polluted by the world (cf. 1:27).

But the tongue's destructive power is seen not only with respect to others but within the lives of the speakers themselves. Under the destructive power of the evil one who seeks to undermine true friendship with God and engender an adulterous love of the world (cf. 4:4-7), the tongue is 'set on fire by hell' (3:6). Left to itself, without the purifying work of the Spirit (cf. 4:5) and the influence of God's gift of true wisdom (cf. 3:15), the tongue will in fact set on fire 'the entire course of life' (3:6) of the speaker. In this way, an unbridled tongue will undermine true religion (cf. 1:26-27) and pollute the speaker by 'staining the whole body' (3:6). This is of course the very opposite of God's good purpose, which, as James made clear right at the outset of the letter, is to bring each believer toward maturity and perfection (cf. 1:4, 3:2).

The fourth and final analogy concerns the total inability of each person ultimately to control the tongue, which is worse than even the wildest of beasts (3:7, 8). In brief, the tongue is untameable, a 'restless evil, full of deadly poison' (3:8b). The restless nature of the tongue points to the fact that, like a caged but wild beast, the tongue is constantly seeking opportunity to break free of restraint, with deadly consequences for all in its path. The phrase 'full of deadly poison' describes the toxic nature of misused words and the terrible capacity that we have as human beings to break down and destroy through our words. But of course, given what James said earlier about the tongue's effect on the speaker, this 'deadly poison' affects the heart and mind of hearer and speaker alike!

A window onto the heart (3:9-12)

In the final section of our passage, James turns his attention to the strange but very real dichotomy within human speech – namely, the ability to both praise and curse (3:9, 10). The praise in view is praise for 'our Lord and Father'

(3:9), presumably as part of prayer and worship. Such praise for God is a normal part of all true religion and, when sincere rather than formalistic, springs from a heart that is dedicated to God. But our human tragedy is that the same mouth that can utter praise for God can, in the next breath, curse a person who is made 'in the likeness of God' (3:9). James does not specify exactly what kind of curses are in view, but in the light of 3:13–4:2 it seems reasonable to assume that these curses were uttered in the course of a personal quarrel and dispute and that they were driven by bitter jealousy, anger, greed and covetousness. In terms of the heart, such curses were a clear evidence of 'double-mindedness' (4:8; cf. 1:8).

Tragically such 'double-speak' is all too common. But this does not mean that James is happy to let it go. In 3:10-12 he strongly asserts that 'these things ought not to be so' (3:10), especially among those who are brothers and fellow believers. James' statement 'these things ought not to be so' is not a claim that believers will never fail in this area but rather a declaration that this kind of 'double-speak' among believers is incongruous and should not be tolerated. The incongruity of such 'double-speak' among believers is seen in the imagery that James uses, drawing once again on the wisdom tradition. No spring 'pour[s] forth from the same opening both fresh and salt water', nor, as James' rhetorical questions show, 'can a fig tree … bear olives, or a grapevine produce figs' (3:11, 12). The lesson from nature is that such 'double-speak' is a clear sign of double-mindedness, or at best of spiritual immaturity. This provides a further reason why believers, especially those who are still immature, should not be too quick to become teachers of others.

From text to message

Given the power of words both for good and for harm, it is tempting, in preaching James 3:1-12, to address the issue of the tongue and our words in general terms. James, however, is addressing not speech in general but the use of words in teaching others, and this should be kept in mind as we teach this passage. Although some commentators restrict James' comments to those who were formal teachers within the community, it seems preferable to take these words as a warning to all who seek to teach others, whether formally or informally. This every member word ministry is of course a great blessing and should be fostered and encouraged. But the content of such word ministry is no less important than the content of sermons preached from the pulpit. And so James' warning stands and remains important. Those who teach will be judged more strictly and, given our imperfect hearts and the reality that we all stumble in what we say, we should not be quick to teach others. This is particularly applicable to those who are still young in the faith and whose zeal may well outstrip their knowledge. At the same time, James' warning against overzealous would-be teachers is a timely reminder that all of us should weigh what we hear and not believe everything that is taught. This point is also worth making as we preach this passage.

Getting the message clear: the theme

Words, though precious instruments that can be used to build up, have the power to do great harm both personally and corporately.

Because teachers will be judged more strictly, because we all stumble in our words from time to time and because words are powerful for good but especially for ill, the role of teaching others should be restricted to those who are spiritually mature.

Getting the message clear: the aim

To encourage believers not to presume the right to teach others but to leave this important task to those who are more mature in the faith.

To encourage believers to pursue maturity so that our words to each other may indeed instruct in the truth and build up rather than mislead and break down.

To remind all of us of the importance of weighing everything that we hear against the truth of the apostolic faith.

A way in

One way in could be to speak about the importance of words for our relationships and the power of words, either for good or for ill, in our own experience. If this is true in general, then how much more relevant and important it is when it comes to words of spiritual instruction. It is for this reason and in the light of our own fallibility that James urges each believer not to be too quick to teach others.

Another way in could be to speak about the value of every member word ministry in seeking to build a culture of disciple-making disciples. But this notwithstanding, there are certain principles and warnings that apply when it comes to word ministry. James 3:1-12 gives those warnings and lays down those principles so that the whole body of believers may indeed grow toward maturity.

Ideas for application

- Presumption is never a good quality within a believer.

- Though zeal to speak gospel truth is to be encouraged, the primary qualification for those who want to teach others is maturity in the faith.

- In teaching truth, as in everything else, believers should be quick to listen to God's truth and slow to speak their own opinions. We need to listen well before we can teach others.

- The way we speak to others is a window onto the state of our own heart.

- Because words are powerful and because everyone is fallible, we should weigh what we hear very carefully indeed.

Suggestions for preaching

Sermon

Undivided (Talk 8)

'Words! Words! Words!' (James 3:1-12)

1. Introduction

   • The importance of words
   (Words are the stock-in-trade of relationships and thus matter a great deal. And what is true of our relationships with others is also true of our relationship with God.)

   • The power of words
   (Words have great power both for good and ill. Words can build up and instruct, but they can also mislead and break down. This is all the more relevant when we remember that we are fallen people and our words are not always edifying.)

2. A reasoned prohibition (3:1-2)

- 'Not many of you …'

  (Because James is aware of the importance of words and our human fallibility, he warns those who are quick to teach others to think twice about whether they in fact should do so. No one is perfect in what he or she says, but those who are mature in the faith can in fact be an encouragement to others through their teaching. James does not say that no one should teach but that not many should.)

3. Four striking analogies (3:3-8)

- Like a bit and bridle …
- Like a rudder …
- Like a spark …
- Like an untamed beast …

  (These four analogies work together to underline James' point that the tongue has a power far beyond its size. And when turned to evil or destruction, its force is devastating – in its great boasts; in its destructive, searing effect on hearer and speaker alike; in its unruly nature and in its ability to poison others' hearts as well as one's own.)

4. A window onto the heart (3:9-12)

- 'Double-speak'

  ('Double-speak' – blessing and cursing – among believers should not be tolerated. If believers habitually speak in this way it is a sign that they are unqualified to teach others.)

- A lesson from nature

  (James' examples of water from a spring and fruit from a tree or vine underline the fact that 'double-speak' is a sign of a divided heart and double-mindedness. Where

this is evident, it is a sure sign of the need for change and a disqualification from teaching others.)

5. In conclusion

- Don't presume.
- Pursue growth so that your words may indeed edify.
- Take care how you listen.

Suggestions for teaching

Questions to help understand the passage

1. What is the only command in 3:1-12?

2. What two reasons does James give to support his prohibition of 'many' becoming teachers?

3. How do the four analogies that James uses in 3:3-8 support his prohibition in 3:1?

4. James' language in 3:5-8 may seem to be exaggerated. Why do you think he speaks in such strong terms in these verses?

5. How does James' reference to the spring, the fig tree and the grapevine point to the problem of double-mindedness that is of such concern in the book as a whole?

6. How does James' teaching in this passage help us to identify who should become teachers?

7. What are the implications of James' teaching in this passage for those who listen to teaching?

Questions to help apply the passage

1. How do you think James' prohibition against many becoming teachers applies today?

2. How does this prohibition not undermine a proper concern for every believer speaking truth to each other for the building up of the body?

3. How would you use James' argument in this passage to encourage believers to identify and deal with double-mindedness so that they can grow toward maturity?

4. In what way would you use James' teaching about the tongue to commend the gospel to someone who is not yet a believer?

5. In what way has James' teaching in this passage surprised, rebuked or encouraged you?

6. What is your prayer response to James 3:1-12?

9.
Wisdom for Life
(James 3:13-18)

Introduction

Right at the beginning of his letter, James urges his readers to ask God for wisdom, especially in the midst of trials. This encouragement to ask for wisdom, along with the assurance that God gives wisdom to all who ask in faith, is a clear indication of just how important this gift of wisdom is for those who want to live wholeheartedly for God. In 3:13-18, James returns to the theme of wisdom and warns his readers that, just as with religion and with faith, there is a choice to be made. On the one hand, there is true wisdom – the wisdom that comes from above (3:15), the wisdom that God gives. On the other hand, there is pseudo-wisdom – wisdom from below, earthly wisdom that, for all its natural appeal, is in reality diabolical in origin. For James the authentic and mature Christian life is the life governed by wisdom from above. Thus, just as he urges his readers to ask God for true wisdom (cf. 1:5), he now warns them of the dangers of being ruled by earthly wisdom. James contrasts the radically different way of life that flows from each.

Listening to the text

Context and structure

As we noted in our discussion of 3:1-12, there are good reasons for seeing 3:13 as the start of a new section. The wisdom imagery in 3:11-12 gives way to direct references to wisdom (3:13 (twice), 15, 17), and the use of a question to begin a new section is characteristic of James (3:1; cf. 2:14; 4:1; 5:13). The repetition of the word 'wise' or 'wisdom' shows that this is the primary theme of the passage, and the comparison of these two types of wisdom (itself a feature of wisdom genre) serves as an invitation to the reader not simply to compare but to choose between them. Of course, part of making the right choice involves listening to the right counsel, so 3:1-12, with its counsel to would-be teachers and implicit reminder to take care how one listens, does have a thematic connection with 3:13-18. This connection is underlined when we note that 3:13-18 continues the focus on words as a window into the heart (3:14).

Some commentators view 3:13–4:3 as a unit, noting especially the reference to 'peace' in 3:17 and 18, in stark contrast to the 'quarrels' and 'fights' of 4:1-2. But the use once again of a question (4:1) to begin the section, the total absence of the word 'wisdom' in 4:1-3, and the stark rebuke in 4:4 that has its antecedent in 4:1-3 all suggest that 4:1-3 connects more closely with 4:4 and following than with 3:13-18. The contrast between 'peace' and 'quarrels and … fights' is then taken as another example of James' use of link words or connected themes to transition from section to section.

Working through the text

An inviting question (3:13)

James' question 'Who is wise and understanding among you?' (3:13) is an invitation to each of his readers to evaluate his or her own spiritual maturity. In 1:5-8, James reminded his readers of the importance of wisdom but also tied the receipt of God's gift of wisdom to wholeheartedness and true faith. The double-minded man, said James, will not receive anything from God (1:7). A life governed by earthly wisdom is therefore a symptom of double-mindedness. But a life governed by 'wisdom from above' is a sign of wholehearted faith and of the growing spiritual maturity that James desired for each believer.

However, James' inviting question raises another question – namely, how will someone know if he or she does indeed have true wisdom? This question is answered by James' exhortation in 3:13 for each one to show the true nature of their wisdom in works of good conduct. Like true faith (cf. 2:14-26), true wisdom is evidenced in works and, in the context of the community, particularly in meekness toward others (3:13). True wisdom is humble wisdom in practice, and it is this point that James stresses in the rest of the passage, by contrasting the 'wisdom from above' with the wisdom that is 'earthly, unspiritual [and] demonic.'

The two ways (3:14-18)

The way of life James describes in 3:14 and 16 is the very opposite of that which comes from a heart fully dedicated to God and ruled by His wisdom. It arises from a heart tainted by 'bitter jealousy and selfish ambition' (3:14), a heart ruled by 'self' rather than by God's word of truth.

Out of such a heart come boasting and falsehood (3:14), as well as 'disorder' and 'every vile practice' (3:16).

The boasting that James refers to here, unlike that mentioned in 1:9, is entirely negative. It is the result of arrogance and is itself evil (cf. 4:16). As 4:13 makes clear, it is an attitude that arises from worldly success and wealth and thus is commonplace among those who see life through the eyes of this world and its wisdom. The problem comes however when it is found among those who should know better thanks to God's truth. When such boasting is found among them, it is a sure sign that they are falling prey to double-mindedness and are being governed not by God's truth but by the lies of the world. And behind such lies we find the influence of the devil (cf. 4:7). Thus, James describes this so-called wisdom that leads to such selfish ambition and boasting as 'demonic' rather than just 'earthly' (3:15).

The word translated 'disorder' is the same word that James used in 1:8, describing the double-minded man as *'unstable* in all his ways'. It is the antithesis of a life of peace or wholeness. The unstable person, like the wave upon the sea (1:6), is blown this way and that by the wind of desire and personal ambition. And this in turn, as James made clear in 1:15, leads to 'every vile practice' (3:16). This phrase is striking and deliberately wide in scope. It points forward to the 'multitude of sins' in 5:20 and serves as a solemn warning that those who seek to follow the wisdom of the world will tread a dark and bitter path, a path that in the end leads to death (cf. 1:15). It is from such a path that James wants to turn his readers (cf. 5:20).

James' warning is important, but by itself it is insufficient. For James' desire is not merely that his readers turn from the path of folly that is disguised as the wisdom of the world. His desire is that they should turn back to the path of truth and to the wisdom from above. He thus ends this section of the letter by pointing to this wisdom and its fruits. These fruits are 'good' and are manifested in certain attitudes and actions: 'pure', meaning unmixed; 'peaceable' rather than unstable and divisive; 'gentle' rather than arrogant and aggressive; 'reasonable' and thus willing to listen rather than being self-opinionated and stubborn; 'merciful' rather than self-serving and callous; 'impartial' rather than judgmental; and finally 'sincere' rather than hypocritical. This last term takes us back to where the list began, to the need for a sincere and undivided heart. From such a heart, led by wisdom from above, springs not disorder and every vile practice but rather peace and a harvest of righteousness (3:18). This harvest of righteousness is, as we have already seen, the very thing that God desires, and the very thing that human hubris and arrogance cannot attain (cf. 1:19-20). It is the 'good fruits' that the Lord produces in those who persevere in following His wisdom, even in the midst of the trials of this life.

From text to message

Given its opening question and its focus on wisdom and good conduct, James 3:13-18 provides an important opportunity for self-reflection in a world filled with noise and distraction. There are many voices clamouring for our attention, all offering their own wisdom as the path to the good life. Some of these voices echo what we heard as we were growing up and seem strangely familiar. Others are quite new and exciting, yet unsettling at the same time. In the end we must choose to whom we will listen and what path we will follow. And it is here that James 3:13-18 helps us. This passage not only invites us to self-reflection but also provides a clear vision of true wisdom, enabling us to choose not just the best, but the right path. And of course, in typical James fashion, it does so by looking beyond our outward conduct to our attitudes and motives and thus to the state of our hearts before God.

In preaching this passage, then, it is important that we keep not only James' theme but also his aim in mind. A sermon on this passage should not simply be instruction about which wisdom is true and which path is worth following, but an urgent invitation to self-reflection and to wholehearted commitment to following God's good path.

Getting the message clear: the theme

True wisdom is the wisdom that comes from above as a gift from God to His people. This wisdom is evident in the good life – a life characterised by humility, righteousness and peace.

The wisdom of the world is ultimately diabolical. It produces a chaotic and self-centred life that brings division and ungodly conduct.

Getting the message clear: the aim

To encourage believers to engage in honest self-reflection and to commit themselves afresh, with the wisdom that God gives, to the way of humility, righteousness and peace.

A way in

Given the wisdom theme in this passage, one way in could be via the question, 'What is the good life?' This is an important question, for the way we answer it will shape the life choices we make. It is also a question to which many conflicting answers are given. And it is a question that requires us to stop and think, to evaluate our own understanding of life and the wisdom by which we live it. James 3:13-18 encourages us to do this honest self-evaluation, but, more than that, it gives us a standard by which we can decide upon a pathway that is worth following.

Another way in could be to speak about the difficulty we all face in finding time to stand still and to take stock of what truly controls our lives. Such reflection is important, but it is something that is hard to do in this busy and distracting world. James 3:13-18 provides us with that opportunity by asking an important question and confronting us with an important choice. It is designed to make us think but also to lead us in the path of God's true wisdom. It is thus a passage that each of us should take to heart and act upon.

Ideas for application

- Self-reflection is an important but often neglected discipline.

- For self-reflection to be worthwhile, we need a standard against which we are to evaluate our opinions and choices.

- The wisdom of the world is natural to us, and to resist it we must consciously choose a different path. God's wisdom is a gift, and it is freely given to those who ask for it.

- The wisdom we choose to follow will always express itself in the way we live.

- The way of life that God's wisdom produces is radically different from that which flows from the wisdom of the world.

- God's way is the truly good life. It is the way of righteousness and peace that flows from putting God and others, rather than self, first.

Suggestions for preaching

Sermon

Undivided (Talk 9)

'Wisdom for Life' (James 3:13-18)

1. Introduction

   - Time to think!

     (In a busy world full of distractions, we seldom take time to stop and think, especially about what motivates and guides our life choices.)

   - Time to choose!

     (There are many voices around us, many options for the so-called 'good life'. In the end we need to make a choice about which voices we will follow and which paths we will choose.)

2. An inviting question (3:13)

   - Am I truly wise?

     (James' question 'Who is wise and understanding among you?' is really an invitation to take stock and ask, am I truly wise? This is a vitally important question because so much is at stake in terms of the life choices we make.)

- What does my life reveal?

  (The kind of wisdom that we follow will manifest itself in the way we live. Thus, we will only know if we are truly wise by looking at how we live. And here 'humility' is the key indicator of true wisdom.)

3. The two ways (3:14-18)

   - The way of the world (3:14-16)

     (The way of the world is a way of life governed by the wisdom of the world. It comes naturally to all of us but should be resisted by believers. It is characterised by bitter jealousy, selfish ambition, boastfulness, instability and a host of sinful actions. In the final analysis it is a way of life characteristic of those under the influence of the evil one. When this way of life is seen among those who profess faith, it is a sign of hearts that are divided rather than fully devoted to God. This is a clear sign that they need to repent and return to God and His wisdom.)

   - God's good way (3:17-18)

     (God's good way is the humble and righteous way of life that He desires each of His people to follow. It is characterised by wholehearted devotion, a commitment to unity and harmony, gentleness, humility and a willingness to learn, mercy, and impartiality, and it is filled with the good fruit of a righteous and godly life. It is the way of God's wisdom at work in the life of the believer.)

4. Conclusion

   - An invitation to take stock!
   - The need to choose!

     (In conclusion and in the light of James' words, each one must ask the question of himself or herself and, more

*importantly, must recommit to God's good way, which
is the way of true wisdom.)*

Suggestions for teaching

Questions to help understand the passage

1. What is James' purpose in his opening question in 3:13?

2. How is true wisdom seen according to 3:13?

3. What characterises the heart ruled by worldly wisdom according to 3:14?

4. How is worldly wisdom seen in practice?

5. What actually lies behind worldly wisdom?

6. What are the hallmarks of a life governed by wisdom from above? (3:17-18)

7. How does this way of life differ from that governed by the wisdom of the world?

8. How does James' teaching in this passage fit in with his concern that his readers should be wholehearted rather than double-minded?

Questions to help apply the passage

1. In what ways do you think James' opening question can help us to take stock of our own values and priorities?

2. Why do you think humility is singled out as a characteristic of godly wisdom? How does this challenge the wisdom of the world?

3. Compare and contrast the characteristics of earthly or worldly wisdom with those of wisdom from above. What conclusions can you draw about your own heart before God from this list?

4. What are some of the things that need to change in your own attitudes and actions in the light of this list? How will you set about this change?

5. There is a strong relational element in James' list of the fruits of godly wisdom. Why do you think this is so?

6. What is your prayer response to James 3:13-18?

10.
Wholehearted Christianity
(James 4:1-10)

Introduction

Throughout the first three chapters of his letter, James' concern has been to hold a mirror of truth before his readers so that they in turn can look into it, not as hearers who forget but rather as doers who act and are thus blessed in their doing (cf. 1:25). To this end and in a rich diversity of ways, James has placed before his readers a picture of true Christianity, a Christianity that is not merely seen in practice, as important as this is, but is also wholehearted. Indeed, it would be closer to James' own conviction to express this as a Christianity that, because it is wholehearted, is thus also seen in the way in which people treat and speak to and about one another and in a living faith that both hears and does God's word of truth. It is to this central theme of wholehearted Christianity and its practical expression that James returns in 4:1-10.

Listening to the text

Context and structure

Both the use of a question and the switch from the third- to the second-person form of address show that 4:1 begins a new section of the letter. The connection with what has gone before is seen in the contrast between the 'peace' mentioned in 3:18 and the 'quarrels and ... fights' of 4:1. But, as we noted in our discussion of the context and structure of 3:13-18, the total lack of any reference to wisdom, the main theme of 3:13-18, shows that the shift from peace to quarrels and fights, is once again James' use of linking material to move from one section of his letter to the next.

Structurally, the passage is complex. 4:1-6 consists of a combination of challenging questions and strong rebukes, which paints a less than flattering picture of the community. The mention of God's grace in 4:6, however, suggests that the situation, though serious, is not entirely hopeless. In 4:7-10 there is a string of imperatives, showing that the primary aim of the passage is to bring about a change, both in attitude and behaviour. But this change in attitude and behaviour is much more than a mere moral reformation. The repeated calls for humility before the Lord in 4:7a and 4:10 arise out of the promise of grace for the humble in 4:6. These in turn bracket the call for heartfelt repentance in 4:7b-9. James' emphasis in this passage is thus on the need for a wholehearted return to the Lord on the part of those whose double-mindedness has led them to flirt with the world, with disastrous results for themselves and the believing community.

Finally, we note the change of theme from division within the community and double-mindedness toward the

Lord (4:1-10) to the problem of harsh judgmental attitudes within the community (4:11-12). This change of theme, together with the form of address 'brothers', shows that 4:11-12 is a new, albeit brief section of the letter. If we note the reference to humility before God in 4:10 and bear in mind that a judgmental attitude and judgmental words flow from a position of playing God over another, then we will see the clear logic of James' moving from humble and heartfelt repentance in 4:1-10 to a rebuke of those who seek to lord it over others in 4:11-12.

Working through the text

A strong but honest diagnosis (4:1-6)

James 4:1-10 begins with two questions that invite the readers not simply to reflect on the current situation within the community, but to look beyond external events to inner attitudes. In view are the 'quarrels and ... fights among you' (4:1), which are the very antithesis of the 'peace' that should have characterised a community governed by godly wisdom and righteousness. James' language, repeated in 4:2, is metaphorical rather than a reference to literal physical fighting. But it is strong and shows his level of concern for his fellow believers. Nor is James content simply to deal with outward conduct, for in 4:1 he identifies the real problem as an inner war of hedonistic passions. It is this inner war of discontentment fuelled by unfulfilled desire that spills over into the fights and quarrels among the believers. Thus, we are back with the problem of the heart that is such a major concern throughout the letter.

As the commentaries make clear, there is debate about the precise structure of James' series of statements in 4:2-3.

I have chosen to follow the ESV rendering which adds
the word 'so' before the verbs 'you murder' and 'you fight
and quarrel.' On this reading, the fundamental problem is
that some within the community 'desire and do not have'
and 'covet and cannot obtain' **with the result that** they
'murder' and 'fight and quarrel' (4:2). Both the strength
of the word 'murder' and the logic of the sentence raise
questions. Surely, if actual physical murder was in view,
this word would have been placed after 'fight and quarrel'
rather than before. And if physical murder was in view
would James not have far more to say? And yet, if physical
murder is not in view, why include the word at all?

Here it is worth remembering that this is not the first
time that James has spoken about murder in relation to
the community's conduct. In 2:11 he used the same word
in the context of a rebuke regarding partiality and a lack
of love for neighbour. Furthermore, the broader context,
with its focus on the inner person (4:1) and heart (4:8),
provides help. For Jesus reminded His disciples that all
manner of evil, including murder, comes out of the heart
(Matt. 15:18-19; cf. Matt. 5:21-22). By speaking about
murder, James is thus warning about the final outcome of
a life ruled by desire and covetousness, but for the grace
of God. Left to ourselves and ruled by our own worldly
desires, we will, in the end, destroy all who stand in the
way of our getting what we want!

Nor is the problem simply a matter of frustrated desire
and community discord. James reminds his readers of a
basic but forgotten truth – namely, that everything good
comes from the Lord and those who do not have should
simply ask. God is, after all, the generous giver to all who
ask in faith (cf. 1:5). Therefore, those who do not receive

God's good gifts either have not asked or have asked with
the wrong motive. It is this latter situation that James
singles out, pointing out to his readers that the asking of
at least some of them is not for the sake of God and His
righteousness, but for the sake of 'the wrong' – that is, for
the sake of satisfying the hedonistic passions that rule their
hearts and cause such strong divisions and dissension (4:3).

If James' honest, though strongly worded, assessment
in 4:1-3 is designed to awaken his readers to their spiritual
danger, then his words in 4:4-6 are designed to shock them
into action. James begins with a stark outburst: literally,
'Adulterers!' (4:4). Gone is the reference to 'brothers',
even though it is clear from the context that James still
considers his readers to be part of God's people, no matter
how compromised they may be. But too much is at stake
for James to mince his words. Indeed, in this passage James
is at his most prophetic, drawing on classic Old Testament
language to rebuke God's people for their spiritual adultery
and idolatrous love of the world. In this, as always, he
speaks for the one whose servant (cf. 1:1) and messenger he
is – namely, the God who gave both physical and spiritual
life to His people and who longs with holy jealousy that
they should serve Him wholeheartedly and not share their
devotion with a rival (4:5).

And the rival here is that most common and most
attractive of suitors – namely, the world, with all its appeal
to our hedonistic passions (4:3). Like Elijah of old (cf.
1 Kings 18:20-40), James calls upon God's people to act
upon what they know but seem to have forgotten. Either
God is God, or the world is god. One cannot befriend the
one and at the same time befriend the other, for 'whoever
wishes to be a friend of the world makes himself an enemy

of God' (4:4). The proud, who seek to serve the world, will be opposed by God. But the humble – who, for all their weakness, turn to God in repentance and faith – will discover that despite His righteous jealousy (indeed, *because* of His righteous jealousy) God gives grace to all who seek to come back to Him (4:6). It is precisely this certainty of grace for the humble that opens the door for James' urgent appeal for heartfelt repentance. And those who heed it, though they turn their back on the love of the world, will find God's righteousness to be an ally, and themselves, like Abraham to be friends with God (cf. 2:23).

An urgent appeal (4:7-10)

As we noted above, 4:7-10 is packed with commands and exhortations, showing that the primary aim of this passage is to bring about real change in the reader. The command 'Submit yourselves ... to God' (4:7) arises out of the assurance that God gives grace to the humble (4:6). This shows that the clearest expression of humility before God is found, not in pious words or religious form, but in a genuine submission to His lordship in everyday life. This is the pure and undefiled religion that James wants his readers to follow (cf. 1:26, 27). This link between submission and humility is seen again in 4:10 where James exhorts his readers, 'Humble yourselves before the Lord'.

This command to humbly submit before the Lord raises the question of what such submission will look like in practice. The commands in 4:7b-9 answer that question. First, submission before the Lord involves resisting the devil (4:7b). In context and in the light of 3:15 where the wisdom of the world is seen as diabolical, to resist the devil means to stand against the temptation of the world. But such resistance against the devil and the world cannot be done without the strength and the wisdom that God gives. Second, in order to resist the devil, readers need to 'draw near to God' (4:8), particularly in faithful prayer. Third, echoing the words of Psalm 24:3-4, James urges his readers to true repentance (4:8, 9). Rather than the 'laughter' and 'joy' of sinful, self-indulgent worldliness, they are to mourn their sin and weep before the Lord and so 'cleanse [their] hands'. Rather than the double-minded attempt to serve both God and the world, they are to 'purify [their] hearts' and so return to wholehearted devotion to the Lord.

Nor should those who return to the Lord in this kind of humble submission forget His promises. In 4:6 James has assured his readers that God gives grace to the humble. In 4:7-10 he reminds them of the outworking of God's grace for His people. Those who courageously resist the devil will find that the devil will flee from them, and they will be able to persevere in the face of testing and temptation (4:7). Those who draw near to God will find that He draws near to them and gives them all that they need, including the ability to stand firm (4:8). Those who humble themselves before the Lord will find that, in His time, He will exalt them (4:10), bringing true blessedness to those who remain steadfast (cf. 1:12; 5:11).

From text to message

The person seeking to preach an expository sermon on James 4:1-10 is faced with two challenges. First, there is the challenge of ensuring that the emphasis of the sermon is indeed the emphasis of the text. We are faced with a string of commands in 4:7-10 and so need to decide which of them are primary and which are subordinate to the main point. In the above discussion we have opted for 'humbly submit yourself to the Lord' as the main point of the passage. The problem of 'fights' and 'quarrels' within the community is thus seen as a symptom of the deeper problem of double-mindedness, a problem that can only be resolved by genuine repentance and a return to the Lord in humble submission. Second, there is the challenge of preaching the passage not simply in its own terms, but in terms of the overall melodic line of the book. Here the command 'purify your hearts, you double-minded' is key, but it must be kept in proper relation to the overall exhortation to humble submission to the Lord.

Given the richness of the passage, one may want to deal with it in a number of talks. However, one needs to ensure that each talk is still connected to the overall emphasis of the passage and that those connections are shown in each talk. Perhaps a title like *Wholehearted Christianity* would work well for a short series on this passage.

Getting the message clear: the theme

Division within the community can often be a symptom of the inner struggle with sinful desires of those who are involved.

The cure for double-mindedness and an idolatrous love of the world is heartfelt repentance and a wholehearted, humble recommitment to God's lordship over our lives.

Getting the message clear: the aim

To alert God's people to the real danger of double-mindedness.

To strongly urge God's people toward true repentance and to humble ourselves in wholehearted submission to the Lord.

A way in

One way in could be to speak about the difference between symptoms and cause. While symptoms matter and can be treated, the really important step is to identify and treat the underlying disease. In our passage 'fights' and 'quarrels' are the symptom. But an idolatrous love of the world is the cause, and it is this underlying spiritual disease that James identifies and for which he provides the only lasting cure.

Another way in could be to speak about the importance of wholehearted Christianity, both for the community of believers and for the growth of the gospel in the world. When Christians fall prey to spiritual adultery and seek to serve both God and the world, everyone suffers. The church suffers because such worldliness always brings strife to the community. The believer suffers since they lose the joy of wholehearted devotion and a deep relationship with God. And the watching world suffers because such behaviour simply reinforces the view that the church is filled with hypocrites. James' honest assessment and urgent appeal provide the only way back to such wholehearted commitment for all who are willing to listen and act.

Ideas for application

- Conflict within a believing community is often fuelled by the sinful passions and desires of those who are involved. Our fights and quarrels are often an expression of self-centredness.

- Those ruled by self-centred passions and ambition are either prayerless or self-focused in their prayers.

- One cannot serve both God and the world. To attempt to do so is in fact nothing less than spiritual adultery and idolatry.

- Spiritual double-mindedness has disastrous consequences for all.

- God shows grace to those who come to Him in humble repentance.

- True repentance starts in the heart but always works its way out in how we act.

- God rewards true repentance with His gracious gifts of spiritual strength and blessing.

Suggestions for preaching

Sermon

Undivided (Talk 10)

'Wholehearted Christianity' (James 4:1-10)

1. Introduction

   - Why wholeheartedness matters
     (Most people would agree that being wholehearted matters in things of real importance. This is certainly true in that most important of areas, our relationship with God. Being wholehearted in our Christianity matters for our church relationships since many of our divisions arise out of our own divided hearts. But it also matters in terms of our witness before the world. None of us wants to come across as a hypocrite.)

2. An honest assessment (4:1-6)

   - Facing the real problem

(In 4:1 James confronts us with the uncomfortable truth that our behaviour, which we easily try to justify, is actually a symptom of what is going on in our hearts.)

- Calling things as they are

(We are easily seduced by the world and end up living a double life, with a foot in the world and a foot in the kingdom. Often our prayerlessness or the self-centredness of our prayers is a symptom of this. If we are to get back on track, it is important to see things the way God does and to recognise that God is rightly jealous over us. More than anything, He wants us to be wholehearted in our relationship with Him. This truth about us is often hard to admit, but we can do so with confidence because God shows grace to those who are humble before Him.)

3. An urgent appeal (4:7-10)

   - The main thing

   (Although there is a string of commands in 4:7-10, all of which matter, James' main concern is that each of us humbly submits once more to God's lordship over every area of our lives. This is the big take-home message from the text.)

   - Getting the main thing done

   (Humble submission to God's lordship in our lives starts in our hearts but reaches to every part of what we do. It thus involves 'hand and heart' repentance, perseverance in the face of temptation and the devil's 'worldly' wiles, and confidence that God will indeed reward those who draw near to Him in this way.)

4. Conclusion

   - God's empowering promises

(In this passage James does more than give us an honest assessment of our problem or a clear and urgent command to repent. He also reminds us of God's gracious rewards for those who do return to Him. If we take God at His word, we will find new strength to stand against the devil's temptation, a renewed sense of God's presence and a sure hope of future blessing when the final battle is won.)

Suggestions for teaching

Questions to help understand the passage

1. What particular problem is James using as the springboard for his teaching in this passage?

2. What is the real problem he addresses?

3. What words and themes are repeated in this passage?

4. Identify the statements and commands in this passage. How do they relate to each other?

5. Using repeated words, statements and commands, how would you outline the structure of James' main argument in this passage?

6. In what way does James draw upon Old Testament language and imagery in this passage? What does this tell us about

   • the urgency of James' appeal?

   • James' own purpose in writing this letter?

7. What promises does this passage make? How do these serve James' purpose?

Questions to help apply the passage

1. To what degree is your church community characterised by quarrels and fights?

2. What have you learnt from this passage about the real problem behind many of these?

3. How has this passage challenged you in terms of contentment?

4. How has this passage challenged you in regard to your prayer life?

5. What have you found particularly striking in this passage?

6. In what ways do you need to change in the light of this passage?

7. How would you use James' teaching in this passage to encourage someone else toward wholehearted Christianity?

8. What is your prayer response to James 4:1-10? (Thanksgiving? Confession? Petition?)

11.
Whose World Is It Anyway?
(James 4:11-12)

Introduction

In our discussion of the structure of the letter in Part One, we saw that the theme of divine judgment is important to James. Judgment will be according to God's 'law of liberty' (2:12) by the judge who is 'standing at the door' (5:9). Strikingly, James' main application of this truth is for believers. As we saw in 2:12, believers are to 'so speak and so act as those who are to be judged under the law of liberty' (2:12). In 4:11-12 James returns to the theme of divine judgment. He stresses that there is only one lawgiver and judge (4:12) and believers are therefore to stop judging one another (4:11).

As we shall see, James' affirmation that God is indeed both lawgiver and judge is contrary to modern cultural assumptions. In contemporary culture the focus is largely on self and the right of self-expression. In such a culture, anything that smacks of 'judgmentalism' is rejected in the strongest terms, and 'Who are you to judge me?' is a common question. Strikingly, James asks a similar question, but he does so not by denying but by affirming that there is a lawgiver and judge. In this way, James reminds us that we live in God's world and, ultimately, we are accountable to Him and to Him alone.

Listening to the text

Context and structure

As we noted in our discussion of 4:1-10, the focus on humility before the Lord leads quite logically to James' prohibition on believers judging one another. As we have already seen (e.g. 1:16, 2:1), the pattern of prohibition followed by direct address generally indicates the start of a new section. Thus, we treat 4:11 as the start of a new section. The strong rebuke and change of theme from judgment to arrogant presumption in 4:13 and the shift of focus to 'the rich' in 5:1 mean that 4:13-17 is a separate unit. Thus, we treat 4:11-12 as a unit in its own terms.

Although James often uses questions to begin a new section, only in 4:12 does he use a question to end a section. The effect of this final question is to challenge the reader to self-examination. Each one is to recognise that God alone is the judge and that they have no right at all to judge one another. This serves both to personalise and strengthen the opening prohibition.

Working through the text

A strong rebuke (4:11)

In 4:11 James once again refers to his readers as 'brothers'. Thus, although he has had some very strong things to say to them, he reminds them that they are members of God's family. It is thus out of familial concern for them as fellow believers that he speaks.

James' concern is that some within the community are speaking 'evil' against fellow believers. In 2:4 he rebuked them for becoming 'judges with evil thoughts' because of their biased and unfair treatment of one another. In 4:11 he rebukes them for their 'evil' words – literally, their practice of 'speaking against' each other. The problem is that of critical and judgmental speech, which has great power to destroy the peace of the community (cf. 3:18). Such behaviour is the antithesis of those works done 'in the meekness of wisdom' (3:13), which are – or should be – typical of those who humbly submit to God's lordship (4:7, 10). Hence the need for strong rebuke.

A compelling argument (4:11, 12)

In the remainder of the passage, James gives his readers two compelling reasons why they should not speak to each other in critical and judgmental terms. First, to do so is in fact to set oneself up as lawgiver and thus as judge over the law and its application. Such a position, especially when it comes to God's perfect law, is untenable for those whose actual responsibility toward the law is to do it (4:11). James' point is not of course that the believers should not be concerned if a fellow believer acts in ways that are contrary to what God says. If that were the case, then no one would be able to take action (as James does and encourages others to do (cf. 5:20)) to turn someone back from sin and spiritual wandering. But he is determined to root out self-righteous judgmentalism and the practice of lording it over another. It is for this reason that he stresses the responsibility of each person to do the law for himself or herself, rather than policing others.

The second reason takes us to the central truth governing James' argument in this short passage: the fact that 'there is only one lawgiver and judge' (4:12). In the immediate context it is natural to see this as a reference to God the Father. As we shall see in 5:9, the judge 'standing at the door' is the Lord Jesus, who will judge all things at His coming (5:7). But this does not detract from the fact that ultimately there is only *one* lawgiver and judge, namely God. Indeed, it is precisely because God is the lawgiver that He is qualified to judge.

But there is another fact about God the lawgiver and judge that underlines His unique authority. God the only lawgiver and judge is the one – and, in this context, the only one – who is able either to save or to destroy. The term 'destroy' speaks about the negative consequence of the judgment that the judge Himself executes. In the light of 1:15 and 5:20, it is a reference to spiritual death. The salvation in view is thus salvation from this death (5:20). The surprise comes from the fact that this salvation is accomplished by the same judge who destroys. The point here must be that the judge saves those who, but for salvation, would in fact face the negative consequences of the judgment. Otherwise, another word such as 'justify' or 'exonerate' rather than 'save' would be used.

But even more striking is the fact that James makes this remarkable point about God the judge's saving grace almost in passing. That is because his primary aim in the passage is not to expound the gospel of salvation but to show his readers that they are totally disqualified from sitting in judgment over each other. They are unable to save each other and therefore they may not judge each other.

A humbling question (4:12)

James' strong rebuke and compelling argument leads him to end the passage with a personal and humbling question: 'But who are you to judge your neighbour?' (4:12). In the light of the truth that there is in fact only one lawgiver and judge, the answer to James' question is clear. When it comes to the right to judge others, each of us is in fact a 'nobody'. Only God – the lawgiver, saviour and destroyer – has the right to judge. And so, James' question applies his argument in a deeply personal and individual way. Each of his readers is thus compelled to evaluate his or her own attitude, spoken or unspoken, toward others.

But by using the word 'neighbour', James' question also reinforces his argument about why no one should speak to a fellow believer in critical or judgmental terms. The term 'neighbour' takes us back of course to the 'royal law according to the Scripture, "You shall love your neighbour as yourself"' (2:8). There, James' point was that to show partiality is to break that law and to incur judgment. In 4:12 he reminds his readers via a question that to speak in judgmental terms against a fellow believer is thus also to transgress the 'royal law'. To do this, then, is not just to judge the law but to break it and bring judgment without mercy upon oneself (cf. 2:12-13). It is however also an opportunity for repentance since 'mercy triumphs over judgment' (2:13) and '[God] gives more grace' (4:6). Once again, James is hard at work seeking to turn sinners away from sin and bring them back to the truth, thus fulfilling his main aim in writing.

From text to message

Despite its brevity, James 4:11-12 is a passage worth expounding, both in its own terms and in terms of James' overall purpose in his letter. First, in our self-centred and self-indulgent culture, it is important to be reminded that God is lawgiver and judge and that we are accountable to Him. Admit it or not, like it or not, the world belongs to God, not to us. In our non-judgmental and all-affirming culture, it is worth being reminded that there are standards of right and wrong and that not everything goes. And yet – and this is James' main point in the passage – the recognition that God rules the world and His standards matter does not give anyone the right to be harsh and judgmental toward others. Indeed, quite the opposite.

Second, James 4:11-12 provides an opportunity to look more closely at how a self-righteous and critical spirit undermines God's saving work among His people. Those who are too quick to judge others are often very slow to look at themselves. And the moment we put ourselves in the place of God, we forsake that humble submission before the Lord that helps to keep our hearts aligned with His saving purposes, not only in our own lives but also in the lives of others. When times are tough, as they undoubtedly were for James' original readers, we need to be reminded that loving rather than judging our neighbour is an important part of perseverance in the faith and growth toward maturity.

Getting the message clear: the theme

God is the only lawgiver and judge, the one who alone has the authority to save or destroy.

Because God alone is saviour and judge, a judgmental attitude and a critical spirit among those who profess to be Christians should be strongly rebuked.

Getting the message clear: the aim

To rebuke all self-righteous judgmental attitudes.

To remind believers that God alone is lawgiver and judge, saviour and destroyer, and to show how this truth should influence how we think about and treat each other.

A way in

One way in could be to talk about our prevailing culture as self-centred on the one hand and non-judgmental on the other. The assumption is that the one leads to the other, but the sad reality is that self-centred people are often quite critical and judgmental. James 4:11-12 is countercultural, putting God at the centre and us in our place. The truth is that with God at the centre of our lives, critical and judgmental attitudes give way to genuine love for our neighbour.

Ideas for application

- Critical, judgmental attitudes and words are always wrong.

- The best thing for us is to see ourselves in the light of who God is.

- Only God is the lawgiver and righteous judge.

- God the judge is also God the saviour.

Suggestions for preaching

Sermon

Undivided (Talk 11)

'Whose World Is It Anyway?' (James 4:11-12)

1. Introduction

   - The 'I' world

     (Our prevailing culture is strongly self-centred. In such a culture there is little or no place for God. Certainly, if God is admitted, He needs to be kept in His place.)

   - A harsh world

     (The sad reality is that a self-centred culture is often harsh and critical – certainly of anything with which it does not agree. The contrary voice, especially if that voice speaks for God, is shouted down.)

2. A strong rebuke (4:11)

   - The world in the church

     (The sad reality is that the self-centredness of the world finds its way into the church. When this happens a harsh and judgmental spirit can arise. Of course, the same thing happens when that self-centredness comes cloaked in self-righteousness.)

   - Stern words

     (In James 4:11-12 James rebukes our critical spirit and judgmental attitude. The rebuke is strong, but it is something that we need to hear and take seriously.)

3. A compelling argument (4:11, 12)

   - Putting ourselves in our place

(Being judgmental is often the result of taking ourselves too seriously. We forget that we are not lawgivers but are called to be doers of God's law of liberty. When we put God's law above our own opinions, we learn to see others correctly and treat them with respect.)

- Putting God in His place

  (God alone is lawgiver and judge, saviour and destroyer. We should thus keep God at the centre of our perspective and be humble before Him. This will enable us to see people as He sees them and will better enable us to pursue His righteous and saving purposes in their lives.)

4. Conclusion

  - Who do you think you are?

    (James' question gives us the opportunity to take stock and to put things right. Do we see ourselves or God at the centre? Are we truly seeking to encourage and build up, to love our neighbour as God wants us to? Or are we simply self-centred and self-righteous? What do you need to do in the light of this passage?)

Suggestions for teaching

Questions to help understand the passage

1. What is the significance of James' return to the form of address 'brothers' in this context?

2. What is the central truth around which James structures his argument in 4:11-12?

3. How does what James teaches in 4:11-12 relate to the main theme of 4:1-10?

4. Why, according to this passage, should Christians not be judgmental toward each other?

5. What important truths about God does this passage teach?

6. How does the question at the end of this passage accomplish James' aim in writing?

Questions to help apply the passage

1. In what ways does this passage challenge the prevailing culture?

2. In what ways has this passage challenged or rebuked you personally?

3. What changes do you need to make in the light of this passage?

4. How has what this passage teaches about God encouraged you? And humbled you?

5. How would you use this passage to commend Christianity to someone?

6. What is your prayer response to this passage? (Thanksgiving? Confession? Petition?)

12.
God Willing!
(James 4:13-17)

Introduction

One of the dangers facing those who have been successful in the past is presumption about the future. And one of the clearest ways in which such presumption shows is in the way people speak. In 4:13-17 James addresses those whose business acumen and success have led them to become presumptuous about the future. Unlike the 'rich' of 5:1-6, those whom James addresses seem to be at least nominal believers. In 4:16-17 he suggests that they know better and that their sin lies not only in their boastful, presumptuous talk, but in their failure to do what they know is right. And thus James, with typical pastoral concern, reminds them of who they really are and urges them to be humble before the Lord and commit their plans to Him.

Given that some have read James as a tract that condemns the wealthy, it is striking that in 4:13-17 James at no point condemns business or profit. Nor is he against careful planning and strategy. What James does condemn is presumptuous boasting and arrogant behaviour, acting as if all our success depends on our own plans and efforts rather than God's providence and kindness.

Listening to the text

Context and structure

The change of theme, from judgmental talk in 4:11-12 to arrogant presumption about the future and boastful talk in 4:13 onwards, shows that 4:13 begins a new section in the letter. But speech remains the focus of the paragraph – specifically, the contrast that James draws between what people are saying (4:13) and what they ought to say (4:15). The difference between what the presumptuous do say with what they ought to have said thus invites the readers to evaluate themselves in the light of this contrast.

James recounts four statements that underline how presumptuous these people are about their future plans, namely 'we will go ... and spend a year ... and trade ... and make a profit' (4:13). In contrast to these, he sets the humble saying 'If the Lord wills', which they ought to employ. The shift from the one to the other comes when those who are currently presumptuous come to terms with their own mortality (4:14) and recognise that boastful speech is evil and that failure to acknowledge God in daily planning is sin (4:16-17).

Although 5:1-6 also begins with the words 'come now' (cf. 4:13), the group that James is speaking to is quite different from that addressed in 4:13-17. Certainly, the reference to the 'miseries that are coming upon you', (5:1) seems to point beyond mere material loss to divine judgment. This suggests that James has the unbelieving rich in view as in 2:6-7. Given this change of addressee, we take 5:1-6 to be a separate unit.

Working through the text

You who say! (4:13-14)

Although it is not immediately obvious, the words 'come now' (4:13) are more than an invitation. These words are a demand for attention directed at a specific group of people within the believing community. The inclusive and encouraging form of address 'brothers' gives way to 'you who say' (4:13). As we shall see, this does not imply that James views this group as outsiders, but rather that they are in danger of falling prey to the sin of presumptuous and boastful speech (cf. 3:5, 14). James' aim then is to grab their attention and urge them toward repentance.

Having obtained his readers' attention, James lists four statements that characterise the boastful speech of this group. The effect of these statements is to build up the image of self-assured, arrogant presumption. It is not that James considers going or spending time or trading or making a profit as intrinsically wrong. His problem is with the arrogance that such statements reveal. More particularly, these statements reveal that such people have not yet come to terms with their own mortality and their dependence upon God for life itself! They speak with absolute confidence about tomorrow or the next day as if their future is certain and their lives are guaranteed. But this is by no means the case. And so James reminds them of what they are – mortal, like 'a mist that appears for a little time and then vanishes' (4:14). The point is clear: given their own mortality and the uncertainty of tomorrow, such self-willed, arrogant, and presumptuous speech is not simply inappropriate, it is evil (cf. 4:16).

What you ought to say (4:15)

In place of self-assured, presumptuous statements, James urges a humble recognition that God is in control, not only of the future, but of life itself. Since it is God who determines whether or not we see tomorrow or the next day, the wise and right attitude to future plans is captured in the saying 'If the Lord wills, we will live and do this or that' (4:15). To speak in these terms is a mark of humility and submission to the Lord (cf. 4:7, 10). It also reveals a heart and mind controlled by 'wisdom from above', for, as we saw in 3:13-14, humility rather than boastfulness is the hallmark of such wisdom. Thus, in urging his readers to think and speak in terms of God's will rather than their own, James is calling them to repent of their worldliness and to commit every part of life to the Lord.

As it is (4:16-17)

James ends this section of the letter, as he did the previous section, with an honest assessment of how things actually are. The present situation is that this group 'boast in [their] arrogance' (4:16). In the eyes of the world, such boasting is a mark of self-assurance and determination, something to be commended rather than avoided. But such worldliness does not belong among God's people. The problem, says James, is not simply knowing what is right. Indeed, as in 1:22, he is confident that they do in fact know the 'right thing to do' (4:17). The problem is that, notwithstanding what they know, they fail to do what is right – namely, to make their plans in submission to the will of the Lord. In this they are guilty of 'sin'. And as we have already seen in the letter, sin is a clear symptom of spiritual adultery and double-mindedness (4:8), and, if left unchecked, leads not to the crown of life that God has promised to those who love Him, but to death (1:12-15). Thus, what appears to be such a small thing – namely, presumptuous talk – turns out to be deadly serious. Indeed, from James' perspective, the stakes could not be higher.

From text to message

There is no doubt that the words 'God willing' can easily become formulaic, words that are spoken without careful thought for their true significance. James 4:13-17 is thus a valuable reminder of what these words actually convey and why they matter. In a world where self-assurance is highly esteemed, and where brash, confident talk about goals and objectives is the norm, we do well to take James' rebuke to heart. Valuable though we are to the Lord, we are only human, here today but gone tomorrow. We are like mist! We have no guarantees and no right to be presumptuous. Nor are those of us in ministry immune to this problem. Indeed, such is the fickle nature of our hearts that we can even add 'DV' or 'God willing' to our plans, and yet speak and act as if we are in control. And so, while it matters that we preach this passage honestly and without compromise, it also matters that we take it to heart ourselves and model what it says. In this, as in everything else in ministry, we are called to watch *both* our life *and* our doctrine.

Getting the message clear: the theme
God controls all things, even our very life breath.

God's sovereignty over everything does not nullify our freedom to plan and act, but it does mean that all our plans should be made in genuine submission to His rule. Refusal to do so is sin.

Getting the message clear: the aim

To encourage God's people to serve Him wholeheartedly by subjecting all their plans willingly to His sovereign rule

A way in

One way in could be to talk about our prevailing culture and the value it places on self-confidence. In contrast to this, there is a better way for those who are believers. This better way is not to eschew planning and work, but rather to remember who we are and who God is, subjecting our plans and efforts to His good and gracious will. James 4:13-17 enables us to do just that by placing our confidence not in ourselves but in God.

An alternative way in could be to talk about the danger of presuming upon God. As Christians we can sometimes turn our trust in the Lord's grace and goodness into presumption. 'If the Lord is willing' can easily become 'because the Lord is willing'. This kind of presumption is most often seen in prayerless planning.

Ideas for application

- Because we are fallen, Christians are not immune to being shaped by the world.

- The world values and esteems self-confidence.

- Presumption and boastful arrogance are not Christian values.

- It is wise for us to live life in the light of our own mortality.

- It is right for us to subject all of our plans to God, for He is the giver of life and the ruler over all things.

- The phrase 'God willing' does not express a lack of faith but a proper trust in the Lord.

Suggestions for preaching

Sermon

Undivided (Talk 12)

'God Willing!' (4:13-17)

1. Introduction

   - You can do it!

     (*Despite the fact that, deep down, many lack confidence, our culture is a 'you can do it' culture. Self-confidence and certainty are the currency of success, or so it is claimed.*)

   - Where is the gap?

     (*Although we know that we should be different from the world, the world does from time to time influence how we think. The result is that, as in James' day, we begin to plan and act in the way the world does, with little or no thought of God. Such presumption is always wrong, but, thankfully, passages like James 4:13-17 help us to get back on track.*)

2. The wrong way to see things (4:13-14)

   - We will, we will, do it!

     (*One of the clearest signs of arrogant presumption is the way we speak. We find that the words 'I' or 'we' dominate our conversation. James highlights this problem by helping us hear just how self-centred our talk can sometimes be.)*

- Nothing's going to stop us now!

  (In our arrogance and presumption, we speak as if we control not just events, but life itself. Nothing could be further from the truth. The hard but kind truth is that we are like the mist – mortal and not actually in control of the things that really matter.)

3. If the Lord wills (4:15)

- Truth worth remembering

  (The true cure for our arrogance and presumption is not simply to remember that we are mortal. It is to remember that our lives and every other good thing come from God. God is the one who rules all things, and we should live and speak in the light of this great, liberating truth.)

- Words worth saying

  (The phrase 'God willing' is – or at least should be – more than a pious formula. It is a phrase that reminds us that God is in control, and we can use it sincerely as an expression of our trust in Him. 'God willing' is thus not an indication of a lack of faith. It is the essence of a humble, wholehearted conviction that God rules the world and we do not.)

4. A matter of life and death (4:16-17)

- The ways things are

  (Boastful arrogance is not something to tolerate. God sees it as evil, even though the world thinks it is commendable.)

- What's really at stake

  (As believers we know that doing God's word matters. And this is just as true when the things we are called to do or to avoid run contrary to our culture. We know that we should depend on God and not on our own ingenuity and ability. The path of self-confident arrogance is not a path to life and blessing; it is the way to death. This truth should lead us to repentance while we have the chance.)

Suggestions for teaching

Questions to help understand the passage

1. What purpose do James' opening words, 'Come now', serve?

2. Note the four statements that James lists in 4:13. What do they have in common?

3. According to 4:14, what important fact have people forgotten when they make presumptuous, arrogant plans for the future?

4. What is the cure for presumptuous thinking according to 4:15?

5. How do the words 'if the Lord wills' contrast with the words in 4:13?

6. How does James view arrogant boasting?

7. According to 4:17, why is arrogant boasting and presumptuous planning a sin?

Questions to help apply the passage

1. How is the statement quoted in 4:13 relevant today?

2. How does what James says in 4:14 challenge contemporary thinking?

3. The phrase 'if the Lord wills' can sometimes become an empty saying. Why do you think that is so? How can we avoid this problem?

4. In what ways has James' teaching in this passage challenged your own heart?

5. What did you find striking or surprising in this passage?

6. What are some of the ways in which James' teaching in this passage could be misapplied?

7. What is your prayer response to James 4:13-17? (Thanksgiving? Confession? Petition?)

13.
Exposed!
(James 5:1-6)

Introduction

In 5:1-6 James directs his attention to the rich. But, unlike 1:11 and 2:6-7, where he speaks *about* the rich, he now addresses them directly and in the strongest terms. As in 4:13, James insists on a hearing. The rich are called to pay attention and consider the verdict that James pronounces against them. And the verdict is certainly not in their favour. Exploitative hoarding of wealth and a self-indulgent, luxurious lifestyle have now been brought to light. What they trust in now stands exposed and inadequate. Indeed, the very wealth that was their refuge has now become poison to them and their greatest accuser before the Lord of hosts, who has heard the cries of those who were exploited.

The language that James uses is strong, even shocking. This is fully in keeping with the strong eschatological tone of the paragraph. The actions of the rich have been done 'in the last days' (5:3). Like the treasure they have laid up on earth, they will be found wanting now that the time of the judgment has come. This suggests that the 'rich' in this passage are unbelievers rather than part of the Christian community. If this is indeed so, then James' description of their actions and the outcome of their choices are intended both as a warning and an encouragement for his audience. James reminds his readers that what this world so values is less than worthless in the eyes of the Lord and of no eternal benefit at all. Given how easy it is to envy the rich, especially in times of trouble, this passage would certainly have been a strong reminder to James' audience not to put their hope in worldly wealth or, as we saw in 2:3, to show partiality toward the rich. And, for those suffering injustices at the hands of the wealthy, James' words would no doubt have been an encouraging reminder that the Lord sees and cares and that justice would be done.

Listening to the text

Context and structure

Despite the repetition of the opening words 'Come now' (5:1; cf. 4:13), 5:1-6 is a separate unit. This view is based on the change of audience as well as the change of tone in 5:1-6 compared to 4:13-17. In 4:13-17 James addressed those who were merchants and rebuked their presumption and arrogance. But the tone of the passage, though firm, was still hopeful, offering repentance to those who were willing to listen. In 5:1-6 James addresses rich landowners. His words offer no hope at all. For them, the evidence is irrefutable, the verdict is final and the judgment has already begun. The command 'weep and howl' (literally, 'weep with howling') in 5:1 is followed by a string of statements highlighting their crimes and the failure of their ill-gotten gains to protect against the certain judgment. The charge is clear and underlined in the repeated phrase 'you have' (5:3, 5, 6). Notably, the command to weep is not because of what they have done but because of the misery which is about to befall them. Thus, the paragraph highlights remorse rather than repentance.

In 5:7 James' focus shifts from the 'rich' to the 'brothers', indicating the start of a new unit. The theme, once again, is patience and endurance in the midst of suffering (cf. 1:12). The connection with 5:1-6 is clear, for the suffering includes exploitation by the rich, and the patience that James urges is possible only because, as 5:4 makes abundantly clear, their cries for justice have reached the Lord of hosts.

Working through the text

A striking reversal (5:1-3)

As in 4:13, James' demand to be heard begins this section of his letter. At first glance the audience is only the 'rich', but on reflection we see James' proclamation to the rich is for the benefit of those within the church. As we saw in 2:2, some within the church were tempted to show special preference toward the rich. And undoubtedly there were others, especially among the oppressed and exploited, who harboured deep resentment and even vengeful hatred toward the rich. Both groups needed to hear James' words – the former so that they would not put their trust in riches, and the latter so that they would not give in to the temptation to take the law into their own hands.

James begins by calling upon the rich to 'weep and howl' (5:1). In contrast to 4:8-9, this weeping is not an expression of mourning for sin and the first step in returning to the

Lord. It is a statement that time is up and that the good life lived 'on the earth in luxury and in self-indulgence' (5:5) is about to end. A great reversal will take place, something so sure that James describes it in typical prophetic terms as something that is already happening. They may still be rich, but in the end their ill-gotten gains will prove worthless. The imagery is striking and recalls Jesus' warning not to store up treasures on earth (cf. Matt. 6:19-21): riches that have rotted, garments that are moth-eaten, and gold and silver that have corroded (5:2-3). But the chief reason why the rich are to lament is because of what their hoarding, exploitative lifestyle has done to their souls, poisoning the heart and consuming life like a destructive fire.[1] And so, the very things in which the rich place their trust and confidence will prove to be a testimony against them and highlight the deadly folly of storing up 'treasure in the last days' (5:3).

An irrefutable charge (5:4-6)

Having spelt out the folly and terrible consequences of a life dedicated to storing up treasure in the last days, James now lays the formal charge against the rich. And here it is clear that it is not simply wealth but ill-gotten gain that is in view. Work has been done and wages are due, but they have been kept back fraudulently (5:4). The desperate cries of those so defrauded have fallen on deaf ears. And so James takes up the cause of the innocent and speaks for those whose voice has not been heard – at least not by those who oppress them.

James opposes all greed. But he is appalled that these wealthy landowners are content to live in luxury and self-

---

1. Note that the word translated 'corrosion' in 5:3 is the word for 'rust' or 'poison'. 'Flesh' is metonymy for 'life'.

indulgence and '[fatten their] hearts in a day of slaughter' (5:5). The day of slaughter may be a reference to the terrible pain and suffering that these rich have brought upon the 'righteous person' (5:6) – that is, the worker who does his day's work with honesty and integrity, only to be denied his wages. Given the nature of subsistence living, withholding pay is a virtual death sentence, condemning the person to death by starvation. It is an act tantamount to murder. And, like helpless animals on the day of slaughter, these righteous but powerless people can do nothing to resist (5:6).

But the day of slaughter may also be a reference to God's judgment on those who prosper in their wickedness and thrive in their treachery as, for example, in Jeremiah 12:1-3. Part of James' denunciation of the rich was to remind them that the cries of the exploited had been heard by 'the Lord of hosts' (5:4) – a Hebraism to describe the God of armies who will destroy His enemies. If this is true, then the 'day of slaughter' refers to God's judgment in the last days (5:3) and underlines both the irony and folly of storing up treasure in such a time. Like animals grazing at the trough in an abattoir, the rich indulge in every luxury, little realising that they are moments away from destruction.

From text to message

Throughout his letter, James challenges us about our attitudes and our actions. Our response to times of trial and temptation; the way we speak to and about others; our attitude to wealth and to the rich; our treatment of the poor and marginalised; our worldview and values; the state of our hearts before God – these are all things that matter a great deal to James.

In James 5:1-6, the spotlight is upon the rich and their luxurious, self-indulgent life that is often achieved at the expense of the poor and vulnerable. Of course, those with wealth within the church would have benefited from James' warnings. They, like all employers, needed a reminder that God sees injustice and will judge it in His time. But, as we have noted, James' aim is not primarily to warn or condemn the rich, but to warn all believers against overvaluing wealth or hating those who have it. In preaching this passage, it is imperative to keep this aim in mind.

Getting the message clear: the theme

Life is much more than the possession of things. Therefore, a life spent laying up earthly treasures is an empty, wasted life. Such a life has no eternal value.

God will call us to account for all ill-gotten gains.

Getting the message clear: the aim

To expose the greedy, self-indulgent life of the rich for what it is – empty and under the judgment of God.

To warn God's people against envying or hating the rich.

A way in

How one enters a sermon on this passage will shape the direction of the talk. Given James' aim, it could be worth entering by pointing out the struggle that we have, either in envying the lifestyle of the rich or perhaps in resenting them, especially if we feel that they have exploited us. In this passage, James provides clear perspective and balance so that we may continue to respond in a godly rather than a double-minded way to the challenges of life in a fallen world.

Ideas for application

- For all its promise, worldly wealth cannot satisfy our inner longings.

- The inner emptiness that comes from chasing wealth is a sign that such wealth has no lasting value.

- Those who have pursued the idol of worldly wealth are left in despair when it fails.

- God's judgment will fall upon those who have exploited others for personal gain.

- Because worldly wealth has no eternal value, the rich are not worth envying.

- Those who are robbed of justice in this world can depend on God's righteous judgment.

Suggestions for preaching

Sermon

Undivided (Talk 13)

'Exposed!' (5:1-6)

1. Introduction

   - If I were a rich man

     (Given the value that our world places on money, it is easy for us to envy the truly rich. Like Tevye in Fiddler on the Roof *we are tempted to ask God, whom will it hurt 'if I were a rich man'?)*

   - Blood, sweat and tears

     (For many, their attitude toward the rich is not envy but bitter resentment. This is particularly true for those who have been exploited by the rich and powerful.)

- A better way

    (By exposing wealth for what it truly is and by focusing on God's righteous judgment, James gives us a Christian perspective and so helps us to live with contentment and patience in a fallen and often unfair world.)

2. A striking reversal (5:1-3)

    - Coming up empty

        (James' words in 5:1-3 are a striking reversal of the way that the world sees the life of the truly rich. Those who put their trust in wealth will suffer its inevitable loss, either through the circumstances of this life or when facing death. At the moment of death, we leave everything behind. But even in the midst of a life of wealth, the endless chasing after treasure leaves us empty. The pursuit of wealth is like a deadly poison or a destructive fire to the soul.)

    - A catastrophic mistake

        (For all the folly of a life dedicated to the pursuit of wealth, the greatest mistake of all is to fail to see things as they really are. For we are living in the last days, and in the end it is God, and not our wealth, who will have the final say on the value of our lives.)

3. An irrefutable charge (5:4-6)

    - Cries from the heart

        (The sad truth is that exploitation of the poor remains a problem in our world. The cries of the exploited are frequently shut out, especially by those who are exploiting them. But God sees and hears all. God will answer the cries of the oppressed, and He will see that justice is done.)

- Guilty as charged

  (*In the remainder of our passage, James lists the crimes of those who live in opulent plenty in the midst of a needy world. Such self-indulgent greed cannot be justified and is weighed and condemned by God the righteous judge. The world may put its spin on how things are, but God sees the truth and His verdict is 'Guilty as charged!'*)

4. Conclusion

   - Therefore, brothers and sisters

     (*James' clear exposé of the emptiness and corrupting power of wealth is a reminder of the danger of desiring to be rich. The failure of wealth in the light of the judgment of God is a rebuke and a reminder of what has true worth. But the reminder of God's guilty verdict and certain judgment against those who enrich themselves at the expense of others also frees us from the need for revenge. We may seek redress, but if we are thwarted we know that God is judge and that He will do what is right.*)

Suggestions for teaching

Questions to help understand the passage

1. Why, according to James, are the rich to 'weep and howl'?

2. Based on 5:1-3, what are the miseries that are about to come upon the rich?

3. What charges does James level against the rich in 5:3-6?

4. What, in your opinion, does James mean by the phrases 'the last days' (5:3) and 'a day of slaughter' (5:5)?

5. In light of what James says in 5:1-6, do you consider the 'rich' he is addressing to be believers or not?

6. What do you think James' main point is in 5:1-6?

7. What do you think James' purpose is in 5:1-6?

Questions to help apply the passage

1. In what ways does James' assessment of the rich contrast with the world's view of wealth?

2. What aspects of James' teaching in this passage have you found particularly striking and relevant to your own experience?

3. What, if anything, in this passage has challenged you to personal repentance? What action will you take in the light of it?

4. How has this passage challenged your thinking about what really matters in life?

5. How has this passage moved you toward godliness and contentment?

6. What is your prayer response to this passage?

14.
Hopeful Perseverance
(James 5:7-12)

Introduction

Those of us accustomed to buying food from supermarkets and corner shops have little idea of the challenges that farmers face. The hard work and high costs of preparing the land and planting a crop are just the beginning. Then it is a matter of patience and hope, waiting for rain, hoping that nothing goes wrong and that the harvest will be successful. And next season requires doing it all again! Little wonder then that James should choose the example of the farmer at the start of a passage where the main theme is patience and steadfastness.

As we saw in 1:1-12, steadfastness in the midst of trials is the theme with which James began his letter. Such steadfastness matters, not for its own sake but for the harvest it produces – namely, the fruit of spiritual maturity, seen in wholehearted devotion to the Lord. Having then underlined the need for and nature of maturity in 1:13–5:6, James returns to its key ingredients, patience and steadfastness. In doing so, he sets the scene for 5:13-20, the final paragraphs of the letter, in which he repeats his deep concern for his readers and explains why he wrote to them in such a direct and sometimes even blunt way.

Listening to the text

Context and structure

The command 'Be patient' and the familiar form of address 'brothers' indicate that 5:7 is the start of a new section. The word 'therefore' shows the link between the call for patience in 5:7-12 and the struggles brought about by the conduct of the rich in 5:1-6. Rather than turning to or against the rich, James urges his readers to maintain their hope in the Lord and keep serving him with patience and steadfastness.

James uses three illustrations to encourage his readers to stay patient. These are the farmer (5:7-8), the prophets (5:10-11) and Job (5:11). The repeated references to the Lord in 5:7-11 provide a further incentive for such patience and steadfastness. Hard though it may be, it is worth doing for the Lord and in the light of His purpose.

The command 'Do not grumble' (5:9) is clearly placed within the context of the command to be patient (cf. 5:8, 10). What is not clear is *if* or *how* the command 'do not swear' (5:12) fits within the logic of the paragraph. Certainly, the formula of a command plus the direct address 'my brothers' can indicate the start of a new section (cf. 1:16). But it is hard to see how a new section on oaths fits in at this point in the letter. Alternatively, one could take the words 'above all' as a literary equivalent of 'finally' and include 5:12 with what follows in 5:13-20. But the shift from oaths to the series of questions and the change of theme in 5:13-20 is hard to follow. Nor should the close connection between the warning about judgment in 5:9 and the reference to condemnation in 5:12 be ignored. Thus, it seems best to take the command 'do not swear' as the logical conclusion of the call to be patient in the midst of trials. For impatience and a lack of confidence in the Lord's willingness or ability to bring a resolution can easily lead not just to grumbling but to rash decisions or even overconfident boasting (cf. 3:5). Indeed, such rash action undermines the process of allowing patience and steadfastness to have their full effect, which is a mature, wholehearted faith (cf. 1:4). It is thus little wonder that James should forbid such double-minded and rash oath-taking in his concern for patient endurance.

Working through the text

A call for patience (5:7-9)

James' example of the farmer waiting patiently for the early and late rains to water the precious fruit (5:7) is bracketed by a repeated command to be patient (5:7, 8). The example underlines the main point, which is perhaps easy to miss. The farmer has no control over when the rain will fall but is confident that it will. And so it is with those whose trust is in the Lord and who wait for His coming. We have no control over when the coming of the Lord will be, but we know that it will happen. Because it is certain, the coming of the Lord thus enables patience and steadfastness. But, because it is in the future, it demands patience, not just in the moment but to the very end.

Nor does James want his fellow believers to view this patience as mere stoic endurance. He reminds them and us that the coming of the Lord is 'at hand' (5:8). Jesus spoke about the kingdom of heaven in such terms, calling on His hearers to repent (cf. Matt. 4:17). James uses the fact as an encouragement to his readers to 'establish [their] hearts' (5:8). As we have seen, this concern for the hearts of fellow believers is the primary reason that James wrote to them. In times of trial our hearts can become divided, and we can easily be lured away from wholehearted devotion to the Lord. When this happens, patient endurance is difficult. Thus, one of the keys to patience and steadfastness is to remember the nearness of the Lord and so to feed and strengthen heartfelt faith. This is what James means when he urges his readers to 'establish [their] hearts'.

But the positive call to establish our hearts is not all that is necessary for patient endurance. For patient endurance and perseverance in the faith to happen, we must also refrain from the sin of grumbling. In our worst moments, such grumbling is directed against the Lord; it is a sin that led to the Lord's judgment upon Israel in the wilderness (e.g. Num. 11 and 14). James' Jewish readers would be well aware of this fact. But such grumbling often finds expression in harsh and critical words about and against others. And so James reminds his readers, as he has done before (cf. 4:11-12), that the Lord, the only judge, is at the door (5:9). There is a clear warning in these words, but there is also an encouragement to patience and steadfastness. For the Lord who is 'at the door' is the righteous judge, and He will bring justice for those who are oppressed. Rather than giving in to the temptation to grumble, they – and we – should trust in the Lord.

Examples of patience (5:10-11)

To further encourage his readers to patient endurance in the midst of trials, James draws upon two examples from the Scriptures. First, he points to the 'prophets who spoke in the name of the Lord' (5:10). Their universal experience, says James, was to experience suffering as a result of their faithful preaching. Their commitment to the Lord did not shield them from suffering but led to it! And their suffering was clearly undeserved. And yet, says James, they remained patient in trials and steadfast in devotion to the Lord. From our perspective, knowing the outcome of their lives, 'we consider [them] blessed' (5:11). But at the time they endured suffering, and thus they needed to persevere with patience.

And the same was true for Job, well known for his steadfastness (5:11). During extreme testing, Job was without answers about the cause of his suffering and was frequently tempted to give up. But he remained steadfast, and thus became an icon of patience. And for those familiar with the story, as James' readers were, the final outcome was a marvellous reversal of fortunes. For what seemed to be meaningless suffering proved to be part of God's purpose for Job. The Lord showed mercy and compassion to Job in the end, and Job's steadfastness resulted in a deeper relationship with the Lord than he had ever known before.

Blessing for those who persevere to the end and the accomplishment of the Lord's good purpose – these are two outcomes modelled by the prophets and by Job. Two outcomes about which James wanted to convince his readers. Once again, we return to where James began his letter. In the midst of trials, even trials that seem beyond our understanding, God is at work to show His mercy and compassion to His people and to lead them to the crown of life that He has promised to those who love Him (cf. 1:12).

More than anything … (5:12)

A comparison with Matthew 5:34-37 shows a marked similarity between Jesus' and James' words. In both cases rash oaths are forbidden and integrity of speech commended. What we do find however in Matthew and not in James is the reason why such oaths are forbidden. They are forbidden, says Jesus, because 'you cannot make one hair white or black' (Matt. 5:36). If James drew his words directly from Jesus' teaching, the question is, why has James included this prohibition on oath-taking at this point in the letter?

As we mentioned in our discussion of context and structure, the answer lies in recognising that oaths or vows are a type of rash and presumptuous talk, perhaps even using the Lord's name. The phrase 'if the Lord wills' could quite easily be twisted to be something like 'as the Lord lives'. Such oaths would then be an expression of personal determination to act instead of patient trust in the Lord's intervention. They may even take the form of bargaining with God: 'Lord, if you will, then I will.' And this is where James is using Jesus' teaching about oaths precisely as Matthew did. For the statement that we 'cannot make one hair white or black' is a reminder of our own lack of absolute power and control. And since we do not have that control, we do well to limit our speech to 'Yes' or 'No', 'I can' or 'I can't'. Where we can, we should. But where we can't, we do well to keep our trust in the one who can and to wait patiently for His mercy and compassion to be shown and

His purposes to be fulfilled (cf. James 5:11). Not to do this is to reveal the true state of our hearts, for as 1:5-7 makes clear, double-talk (yes *and* no, rather than yes *or* no) comes from a divided heart. More seriously, speaking this way is to fall into the trap of the 'evil one' (cf. Matt. 5:37) and thus to fall under the Lord's condemnation (5:12).

From text to message

Given our culture's commitment to a life of instant gratification, it is not surprising that virtues like patience and perseverance are in short supply. As the famous Queen song says, 'I want it all and I want it now!' Tragically, there are many who baptise that sentiment into the church via the various forms of the prosperity gospel. More tragically still, there are many who, having been let down by false promises, turn from the counterfeit to no gospel at all.

James reminds us that God's purposes for us are very good, and when they are fulfilled we will indeed be 'lacking in nothing' (cf. 1:4). In the future we will inherit the 'crown of life' (cf. 1:12). But that lies in the future. In the present – and contrary to the world's message – we will face trials and will need to show patient endurance like the farmer, the faithful prophets and Job. Others may grumble, act unilaterally, or perhaps even 'name and claim', but God's true people are called to trust and obey while we wait with eager expectation for our salvation to be fully revealed. Ours is a message of steadfast faith in present suffering followed by glory later – it is the 'adversity gospel'. It is this gospel that James 5:7-12 proclaims as a necessary answer to our world's impatient longing.

Getting the message clear: the theme

The Lord's coming is a future certainty.

In the light of the Lord's coming, believers are called to live with steadfast faith and patience.

Getting the message clear: the aim

To encourage believers to live with steadfast faith and patience as we wait for the coming of the Lord.

A way in

One way in could be to talk about the world's instant gratification culture and how that has also infiltrated the church. In such a culture, patience and steadfastness in trials is a lost virtue. But as believers we are called to be different and to model something better to a needy world. James 5:7-12, though it challenges our culture, in fact provides the message it so desperately needs to hear.

Another way in could be to remind our audience that finishing well is a very important biblical principle. The Bible gives us clear examples of people who started well but who finished badly – King Saul, King Solomon and of course the Exodus generation who perished in the wilderness. In our own experience we can recall people who made a good start in the faith but who then gave up along the way. In James 5:7-12, James reminds us of the importance of patient perseverance to the end so that we will not give up but finish well.

Ideas for application

- Patience and steadfastness are highly valued by God.

- Patience and steadfastness need to be encouraged, especially when trials come.

- When trials come, we are tempted to grumble and to make rash, even arrogant decisions.

- Patient endurance begins within our hearts. If we are to be patient and steadfast, we must strengthen our heart commitment to the Lord.

- Conviction about the Lord's return is key to steadfastness.

Suggestions for preaching

Sermon

Undivided (Talk 14)

'Hopeful Perseverance' (5:7-12)

1. Introduction

   - The 'now' world

     (*Our culture lives for instant gratification. This aspect of the culture has sadly infected the church as well. In such a culture the 'prosperity gospel' flourishes, even in sophisticated, less crass forms.*)

   - The 'now/not yet' gospel

     (*While the gospel does bring us blessing now, it is primarily a forward-looking gospel. We are called to live by faith, not by sight, and with hope for the future. This means that in the present we are called to patient endurance. James 5:7-12 helps us to do that.*)

2. Called to be patient (5:7-12)

   - Examples of patient endurance

(In order to motivate us to patient endurance, James provides three examples: the farmer, the prophets and Job. Each of them needs to be patient in the midst of circumstances beyond their control (the farmer and rain) or undeserved suffering and trials (the prophets and Job).)

- The essence of patient endurance

  (James' repetition of the command 'be patient' shows how seriously he takes this issue. But what does it mean in practice to endure with patience? James has a positive command to give that concerns our hearts, but he brackets that positive command with warnings about behaviour that will undermine patient endurance.)

  - Don't grumble

  - Don't make rash vows and plans in your own wisdom

  - Do establish your heart

- Empowering patient endurance

  (As we look at the passage, we see that our hearts are the key to patient endurance. And we also discover that the key to an established heart is believing truth about the Lord – that He is the judge, He will return, and His coming is 'at hand'. But the Lord is also merciful and filled with compassion. We can thus ask Him for the power to remain patient and steadfast to the end.)

3. Conclusion

- Counterintuitive

  (Even as Christians, we find it hard to remain patient in trials. And yet our passage has taught us that this is our calling in the Lord – it is a mark of true faith.)

- Counterculture

(Hard though it is to be patient and steadfast in trials, let us keep our eyes on the Lord and ask Him for the power to live in this way, as a witness to the world. When we are different from the world, we are most attractive to it.)

Suggestions for teaching

Questions to help understand the passage

1. What words are repeated in 5:7-12?

2. What commands does James give in 5:7-12?

3. How do the repeated words and commands shape the structure of the passage?

4. What key truths about the Lord do we learn from this passage?

5. How do these key truths function to accomplish James' purpose?

6. How, in your opinion, do the commands 'do not grumble' and 'do not swear' tie in with the command to be patient?

7. How does the command 'establish your hearts' enable patience and steadfastness?

Questions to help apply the passage

1. In what ways does James' teaching about patience and steadfastness challenge our culture?

2. What needs to change in your own life as a result of this passage? What practical steps can you take to implement these changes?

3. James frames the call for patience and steadfastness with truths about the Lord and His purposes. Which of these truths is most relevant for you at this moment?

4. Think about the way you speak about the challenges you face. How might that change in the light of 5:9 or 5:12?

5. Think about someone you know who is going through a difficult time at the moment. How could you encourage or witness to them using this passage?

6. What is your prayer response to this passage?

15.

A Call to Spiritual Restoration
(James 5:13-20)

Introduction

Throughout his letter, James has shown a deep pastoral concern for his readers. He has instructed them, warned them, and at times rebuked them strongly. But his goal has always been to protect them from drifting and to build them up to maturity. James' letter is a call to spiritual restoration, made to believers who were under pressure from the world, its trials and its temptations.

Nowhere is James' pastoral concern more clearly seen than in 5:13-20, the final section of the letter. First, in 5:13-18 James sketches a variety of scenarios which provide a springboard for him to revisit key themes raised in the opening section of the letter – especially the role of prayer as the means through which God works powerfully to restore the weak and to keep His people wholehearted and steadfast in faith. Nor is this ministry of prayer for one another the preserve of the few. It belongs to all of God's people – elders and fellow believers alike – who in this particular task are called to emulate Elijah, the righteous man whose prayers God used to bring His people back to Himself.

Then, in the final paragraph (5:19, 20), James reminds his readers that every believer is to be 'his brother's keeper'. Like Elijah who spoke and prayed to bring Israel back to the Lord, James, the servant of God, wrote out of pastoral concern, especially for those who were weak and prone to wander. But this task was not his alone. And so he ends the letter with a reminder to all, that the right response to those at risk of drifting away from the truth is not a self-righteous, judgmental attitude but a deep concern to see them restored.

Listening to the text

Context and structure

The passage begins with three questions (5:13, 14) and ends with a longer wisdom saying (5:20; cf. 1:12). At first glance the various parts of the passage seem to be unrelated; however, as we shall see in our discussion of the text, the central concern of the passage is the spiritual health and full restoration of those who are weak and in danger of drifting away.

The passage can be divided into two parts – namely, 5:13-18 and 5:19-20. The primary focus of 5:13-18 is prayer. This echoes the teaching of 1:5-8 where prayer plays a key role in combatting double-mindedness and enabling steadfast perseverance in faith especially in the midst of trials. Thus the shift to a discussion on prayer (5:13-18) follows logically from the call to steadfastness and patience in the preceding section in 5:7-12. The references to sin in 5:15-16 anticipate the reference to sin and death in 5:19-20. They also echo the warnings of 1:13-15 and remind the readers of what is at stake. The primary imperative in this section is 5:16 – 'Confess your sins to one another and pray for one another, that you may be healed' – that is, be restored (see below). This focus on prayer in the context of repentance and restoration leads logically to the example of Elijah, as a man of prayer whose deep desire was the restoration of wholehearted devotion among God's people.

The statement that Elijah was 'a man with a nature like ours' (5:17) opens the way for James' final comments. Like Elijah, his God-given task is to bring wandering sinners back to the truth (5:19). But this task is not his alone. Every believer is exhorted to 'know' 'that whoever brings back a sinner from his wandering will save his soul from death and cover a multitude of sins' (5:20). This longer wisdom saying combined with the imperative 'know' concludes the letter and summarises its primary pastoral concern.

Working through the text

Is anyone? (5:13, 14)

In the opening verses of the passage, James addresses three scenarios that his readers may face. The first, that of suffering, was common for those 'in the Dispersion' (1:1), subject to 'trials of various kinds' (1:2) in which they are called to remain steadfast (1:12; 5:11). As in 1:5, James' counsel for such remains 'Let him pray' (5:13) – that is, pray for wisdom and strength to stay faithful and steadfast till the end. But also, pray that they will not fall into the sin of double-mindedness and so begin to wander away from the truth (5:19-20; cf. 1:5-8).

Second, for those who are 'cheerful' – that is, have peace of mind – despite the trials they face, James urges songs of praise (5:13). These songs are an expression of gratitude to God for His sustaining power, and they are a reminder that the ability to stand firm in the midst of trials comes not from our own strength but from God. Thankfulness to God is a key aspect of spiritual health.

Thirdly, James addresses those who may be sick (5:14). What follows in 5:14-18 involves a much longer discussion that, given the diversity of interpretations among commentators, we will deal with in a separate section.

What about the sick? (5:14-18)

Speaking personally, I find James 5:14-18 the most difficult passage in the letter. The mention of suffering and peace of mind in 5:13, fits well with the overall theme of the letter. But the reference to sickness has no connection at all to what has gone before and seems totally out of place in the concluding paragraph of the letter. And even if we grant that physical sickness is in view, why – in a paragraph that asserts that we like Elijah can all pray – does James not say, 'If anyone among you is sick, let him pray'? Surely sickness is part of the suffering in 5:13? So why should the elders be called to pray and anoint with oil? And, for that matter, what does the anointing do? Is it symbolic? And if so, of what?

And, as if these questions were not challenging enough, we note the repeated reference to 'sins' in 5:15-16 and the surprising connection between confession of sin and healing (5:16). Does that mean that the particular sickness in view is a result of sin? And if so, why does James say, '*if* he has committed sins' (5:15)? And finally, why should Elijah, of all the prophets, be chosen as an example of prayer, if the problem was physical sickness? In Jewish and early Christian thought, Elijah was the icon of spiritual restoration, not physical healing (cf. e.g. Matt. 17:10-11).

In my opinion, the key to this passage is the way in which we interpret the words 'sick' (5:14) and 'healed' (5:16). The most common use of these words is with reference to physical sickness but there are exceptions. Notably, the word 'sick' (5:14) is translated 'weak' in Matthew 26:41. Jesus had urged His disciples to 'watch and pray' lest they enter into temptation – that is, fail to remain steadfast in the test of faith they were about to face. Returning to find them asleep, Jesus says, 'The spirit indeed is willing, but the flesh is weak.' Clearly human frailty resulting in the inability to carry out an important spiritual task, rather than actual sickness is in view. Furthermore, the word 'healed' (5:16) is used in Matthew 13:15 not of physical healing but of the need for wholehearted repentance leading to spiritual restoration. Jesus is quoting Isaiah 6:9-10 and is referring to the privilege which His disciples have in contrast to the crowd. In Jesus and His word of life, the disciples have been given the secret of the kingdom. The crowd however remain lacking in spiritual understanding and thus in need of God's gift of open eyes and ears and a changed heart.

This interpretation of the words 'sick' to mean human weakness and 'healed' to mean spiritual restoration seems to me to make the most sense in the context. First, it fits well in the closing section of a letter which was designed to urge and encourage believers to remain steadfast and wholehearted in their faith, even in the midst of trials. Second, it explains why the person described in 5:14 should call for the elders to pray. Given the exhortation to 'pray for one another' (5:16), why should the elders be called? But if weakness and temptation to wander away from the truth are in view as in 5:19, it makes sense that the weak person should seek the help of the elders and ask for prayer – not for physical healing but for renewed commitment. Such a recommitment could have been done in the public gathering, but it is not impossible that the weak person should want it to take place in greater privacy, with two or three gathered in the name of the Lord. This would be the ideal opportunity for any particular sins to be confessed (5:16) and for those with spiritual oversight to assure the weak and doubting person of the Lord's forgiveness and restoring power (5:15). It would also be the ideal opportunity for anointing with oil in the name of the Lord (5:14) not as a symbol of God's healing power, but as a symbol of consecration and rededication.

Why Elijah? (5:16-18)

The exhortation to pray for the spiritual restoration of one another leads to another of James' pithy sayings: 'The prayer of a righteous person has great power as it is working' (5:16). In 2:14-26, the righteous person is someone with living faith that expresses itself in works and that is able to save. In 5:16 the work of faith of the righteous man is prayer to God and, in particular, prayer that follows the example of Elijah, the man of prayer (5:17). James describes Elijah as a man with a nature like ours. Given the extraordinary things that God did through Elijah such a statement is hard to believe. But James is not referring to Elijah's calling and authority as a prophet in general, but to his prayer in a very specific context.

This raises two questions, namely – When did Elijah pray? and What did he pray for? In 5:17-18 James speaks about Elijah's prayer for rain. This is an allusion to the events of 1 Kings 18 where Elijah's prayers are recorded. A careful look at Elijah's prayer in 1 Kings 18:36-37 shows five things. First, the prayer comes in the context of Elijah confronting Israel about the problem of their divided hearts (1 Kings 18:21). Second, Elijah prayed that the people, whose loyalty was divided between Yahweh and Baal, would know that Yahweh alone was God in Israel. Third, Elijah prayed that the people would know that he, and not the prophets of Baal, was the true prophet. Fourth, Elijah prayed that the people would know that he had acted in obedience to God's word. Fifth, Elijah prayed that the people would know that it was the Lord, rather than Elijah, who was turning their hearts back to Himself.

The example of Elijah as a man of prayer fits completely with James' pastoral purpose in 5:14-18. As we have already seen (cf. 1:8; 4:8) James was concerned that, like Israel in Elijah's day, his readers were in danger of wavering between two opinions (cf. 1 Kings 18:21). Their faith in the Lord was being tested by trials of various kinds, and some at least had fallen prey to the temptation of trying to serve both the Lord and the world (cf. James 4:4). Like Elijah, and in his prophetic role as a 'servant of God and of the Lord Jesus Christ' (cf. 1:1), James calls upon those who had become double-minded and who were flirting with the world to repent and return to the Lord. And like Elijah the man of prayer, he doubtless practised what he urged others to do – that is to pray for the weak who were in danger of wandering away from the truth to be restored to whole-hearted commitment and steadfast faith.

But James also knew that a key means for the restoration of those who were weak in the faith was the care of the community of believers – care given not only by the leaders, but by fellow believers. Thus he urges those who are weak to reach out to the elders for help (5:14). But he also urges mutual accountability and prayer for one another (5:16). And so doing he invites each believer to be like Elijah – a righteous man concerned for the spiritual well-being of all of God's people.

If anyone (5:19-20)

In 5:19-20 James ends his letter by describing a scenario in which someone in the community of believers wanders (literally, 'is led astray' or 'deceived', as in 1:16, 26) from the truth. The phrase 'if anyone', in the context of a letter, has the sense of 'when' rather than 'if'. The question is what should be done in such a case? And James' answer is clear. When someone wanders away, it is the privilege and responsibility of those who are able to help, to '[bring] him back'. Like Elijah, James has had this purpose in his letter, and it is the reason he has written so forthrightly. In that sense he is the 'someone' who tries to bring the person back. But since Elijah is also a model for every believer (cf. 5:17), this ministry of restoration is a 'one another' ministry (cf. 5:16). James' use of the word 'someone' thus also serves to encourage those who read his letter to share his burden for those who are wandering away and to follow his example in seeking to bring them back from their wandering.

And, as 5:20 makes clear, the stakes could not be higher. In 1:13-15 James warned his readers that those who wander away in the face of temptation will inevitably fall into sin. And sin, if left unchecked, will lead to death. In 5:20 James reminds his readers that action to help the sinner who is wandering from the truth will 'save his soul from death and will cover a multitude of sins'. Of course, only the Lord can forgive sin. But, as 4:6-10 and 5:16 make clear, that is precisely what the Lord will do for those who repent and draw near to Him. In 5:20 James uses this assurance of God's forgiving grace to motivate those who are standing firm in the faith to look past their own salvation and to the salvation of others. In this, they – and we – follow not just James' example but the example of the one who came to seek and to save the lost, our Lord and saviour Jesus Christ.

From text to message

A sermon on the final section of a New Testament letter provides an opportunity for the preacher to revisit and reinforce important themes and applications. The danger is that the sermon simply becomes a recap of the whole letter, rather than an exposition of the specific text. The key is thus to take the opportunity while avoiding the danger.

As we have seen, James 5:13-20 is a rich and difficult passage. The closing words (5:19-20) act as a purpose statement for the letter and are thus a good springboard for speaking about the letter's overall theme. And, as I have tried to demonstrate, their focus on the restoration of a sinner who has wandered away from the truth also fits in with the main theme of 5:13-18. So, in the case of James 5:13-20, a sermon on the text itself does cover the primary theme of the letter as a whole.

Given the different interpretations of 5:14-16, careful attention must be given to the meaning of the words 'sick', 'healed' and 'saved'. It is important not to get bogged down in detail but rather to say just enough to persuade the hearer of the chosen interpretation. Sermons on healing or the role of the elders are, in my opinion, not in line with the theme of the text. In what follows I have thus presented an outline for a single talk on the whole passage, centred on the theme of spiritual restoration.

Getting the message clear: the theme

The spiritual restoration of those who have wandered away from the truth, or who are weak and in danger of doing so, should be a priority for every believer.

Getting the message clear: the aim

To urge God's people to take responsibility, not simply for their own steadfastness in the faith but also for the restoration of those who have wandered away.

A way in

Given the alignment of the theme of the passage and the theme of the letter, one way in to preaching James 5:13-20 could be to talk about why James wrote his letter and why it is so important for us to have studied it together. This could open the door for a brief summary of some of the key lessons learned, but it could also lead to a focus on the main concern – namely, the restoration to wholehearted faith of those who are weak or have wandered away.

Another way in could be to speak about the importance of being wholehearted in our faith, reminding people that from time to time our commitment can become weak. James 5:13-20 reminds us of why such weakness and spiritual double-mindedness is dangerous. But it also gives us real help on how to get back on track with the help of others – and how to help others in a similar situation of weakness. Thus, we are reminded that helping others is one of the best ways of helping ourselves.

Ideas for application

- Prayer and praise to God are of vital importance for a healthy Christian life.

- Those who are feeling spiritually weak and vulnerable should turn to those who are more mature in the faith for help. Spiritual isolation is never a healthy option.

- We can be assured – and assure others – that if we truly confess our sins to the Lord, we will be forgiven.

- Sometimes it is helpful for us to confess our sins to others and to seek their help in getting back on track spiritually.

- God hears and answers the prayers of all His people, for in the final analysis we are all sinners saved by His grace.

- Faithful prayer is effective and thus vital for our own or someone else's spiritual restoration.

Suggestions for preaching

Sermon

Undivided (Talk 15)

'A Call to Spiritual Restoration' (5:13-20)
1. Introduction

- Big lessons from a short letter
(Our study of James has instructed, challenged and, at times, rebuked us in a number of areas that are important for our growth to maturity in faith. Examples are

steadfastness in trials, resistance to temptation, the way we treat and speak to others, and the importance of prayer.)

- The most important lesson of all

  (Important though each of these lessons is in its own right, together they play a role in James' main lesson – namely, the need for us to be wholehearted and undivided in our faith in the Lord. This matters for us as individual believers, but it also matters for our brothers and sisters in the faith. In James 5:13-20, our text for today, it is this most important lesson that will occupy our attention.)

2. An invitation for anyone

   - Prayer and praise (5:13)

     (Those who are suffering are encouraged to pray for wisdom and perseverance. Those who are at peace are reminded to thank God for His grace.)

   - An encouraging word for the spiritually weak (5:14-16)

     (The sick in 5:14 are in fact the spiritually weak. We see this when we look at the words 'sick' and 'healed' in the context of the passage as a whole. James wants the weak to find help and to be restored. This is best done not by cutting oneself off but by seeking spiritual help from those with whom we can be honest about our sins – those who will pray with us rather than judge us.)

3. An unexpected prophet (5:16-18)

   - Elijah, the man of prayer

     (Even though we would never liken ourselves to Elijah, James does. We are called to imitate Elijah and in particular his prayer.)

- Elijah, the restorer of Israel

  (In 1 Kings 18:36-37 we see that Elijah prayed for two things. First, he prayed that Israel would recognise his God-given authority. James wants us to feel the same way about his letter. But second, Elijah prayed that God would restore His people and that they would know that God had done it. We are thus encouraged to pray for our own restoration and the restoration of others, knowing that the Lord is the one who saves and raises up.)

4. Our brother's keeper (5:19-20)

   - Prone to wander

     (Under pressure from trials and temptation, we are prone to wander from the Lord and a wholehearted devotion to Him.)

   - Our brother's keeper

     (The end result for those who wander from the truth is spiritual death. But things don't have to end this way. James' burden for the believers in his day is an incentive for them and for us to be concerned for those who we know are drifting spiritually. This is a great privilege and a great responsibility. But since it is the Lord who turns people back to Himself, it is a task that we undertake with full confidence and commitment.)

Suggestions for teaching

Questions to help understand the passage

1. What groups within the community does James address in 5:13-20? What are the distinctive characteristics of each of these groups?

2. What key words are repeated in 5:13-20?

3. What are the imperatives in 5:13-20?

4. Which imperative would you consider to be the main imperative?

5. What role does the example of Elijah play within the logic of the passage?

6. What purpose does 5:19-20 play

    - within 5:13-20?
    - within the letter as a whole?

Questions to help apply the passage

1. What have you found hardest to understand in 5:13-20?

2. In what ways has this passage surprised, challenged and encouraged you?

3. How has this passage helped you to be steadfast in your faith?

4. In what ways has this passage helped you to appreciate

    - your church community?
    - your church leaders?

5. James 5:13-20 reminds us that we are to help those who may be drifting spiritually. Who can you think of that would benefit from such help? What steps will you take to help them?

6. What is your prayer response to this passage?

FURTHER READING

James Adamson, *The Epistle of James* (Grand Rapids, USA: Eerdmans, 1976).

Peter Davids, *The Epistle of James* (Exeter, England: Paternoster Press, 1982).

Dan G. McCartney, *James* (Grand Rapids, USA: Baker, 2009).

Scot McKnight, *The Letter of James* (Grand Rapids, USA: Eerdmans, 2011).

Douglas J. Moo, *The Letter of James* (Leicester, England: Apollos, 2000).

About The Proclamation Trust

The Proclamation Trust is all about unashamedly preaching and teaching God's Word, the Bible. Our firm conviction is that when God's Word is taught, God's voice is heard, and therefore our entire work is about helping people engage in this life-transforming work.

We have three strands to our ministry:

Firstly we run the Cornhill Training Course which is a three-year, part-time course to train people to handle and communicate God's Word rightly.

Secondly we have a wide portfolio of conferences we run to equip, enthuse and energise senior pastors, assistant pastors, students, ministry wives, women in ministry and church members in the work God has called them to. We also run the Evangelical Ministry Assembly each summer in London which is a gathering of over a thousand church leaders from across the UK and from around the world.

Thirdly we produce an array of resources, of which this book in your hand is one, to assist people in preaching, teaching and understanding the Bible.

For more information please go to www.proctrust.org.uk

Also available in the Teaching Series...

TEACHING THE BIBLE SERIES

OLD TESTAMENT

TEACHING NUMBERS – ADRIAN REYNOLDS 978-1-78191-156-3

TEACHING JOSHUA – DOUG JOHNSON 978-1-5271-0335-1

TEACHING 1 SAMUEL – ANDREW REID 978-1-5271-0532-4

TEACHING 1 KINGS – BOB FYALL 978-1-78191-605-6

TEACHING 2 KINGS – BOB FYALL 978-1-5271-0157-9

TEACHING EZRA – ADRIAN REYNOLDS 978-1-78191-752-7

TEACHING RUTH & ESTHER – CHRISTOPHER ASH 978-1-5271-0007-7

TEACHING PSALMS VOL. 1 – CHRISTOPHER ASH 978-1-5271-0004-6

TEACHING PSALMS VOL. 2 – CHRISTOPHER ASH 978-1-5271-0005-3

TEACHING ISAIAH – DAVID JACKMAN 978-1-84550-565-3

TEACHING DANIEL – ROBIN SYDSERFF, BOB FYALL 978-1-84550-457-1

TEACHING AMOS – BOB FYALL 978-1-84550-142-6

NEW TESTAMENT

TEACHING MATTHEW – DAVID JACKMAN, WILLIAM PHILIP 978-1-84550-480-9

TEACHING MARK – ROBIN SYDSERFF 978-1-5271-0533-1

TEACHING ACTS – DAVID COOK 978-1-84550-255-3

TEACHING ROMANS VOL. 1 – CHRISTOPHER ASH 978-1-84550-455-7

TEACHING ROMANS VOL. 2 – CHRISTOPHER ASH 978-1-84550-456-4

TEACHING EPHESIANS – SIMON AUSTEN 978-1-84550-684-1

TEACHING 1 & 2 THESSALONIANS – ANGUS MACLEAY 978-1-78191-325-3

TEACHING 1 TIMOTHY – ANGUS MACLEAY 978-1-84550-808-1

TEACHING 2 TIMOTHY – JONATHAN GRIFFITHS 978-1-78191-389-5

TEACHING JAMES – *MERVYN ELOFF* 978-1-5271-0534-8

TEACHING 1 PETER – ANGUS MACLEAY 978-1-84550-347-5

TEACHING 2 PETER & JUDE – ANGUS MACLEAY 978-1-5271-0563-8

TEACHING 1, 2, 3 JOHN – MERVYN ELOFF 978-1-78191-832-6

PRACTICAL PREACHING

BURNING HEARTS – JOSH MOODY 978-1-78191-403-8

BIBLE DELIGHT – CHRISTOPHER ASH 978-1-84550-360-4

HEARING THE SPIRIT – CHRISTOPHER ASH 978-1-84550-725-1

SPIRIT OF TRUTH – DAVID JACKMAN 978-1-84550-057-3

TEACHING THE CHRISTIAN HOPE – DAVID JACKMAN 978-1-85792-518-0

TRANSFORMING PREACHING – DAVID JACKMAN 978-1-5271-0692-5

THE MINISTRY MEDICAL – JONATHAN GRIFFITHS 978-1-78191-232-4

THE PRIORITY OF PREACHING – CHRISTOPHER ASH 978-1-84550-464-9

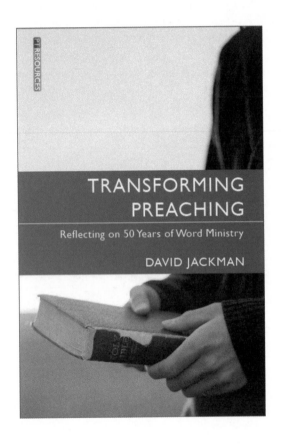

TRANSFORMING
PREACHING

Reflecting on 50 Years of Word Ministry

DAVID JACKMAN

978-1-5271-0692-5

Transforming Preaching

Reflecting on 50 Years of Word Ministry

David Jackman

In *Transforming Preaching*, David Jackman, reflecting on over fifty years of Word ministry offers real encouragement and help with some of the ongoing challenges and pitfalls facing the preacher. Each chapter addresses a different theme that will shape and sharpen the reader in their thinking about what it means to be a faithful expositor and servant of the Word.

It must be nearly impossible for a book on preaching by David Jackman (reliable, proven, full-orbed preacher that he has been for fifty years) to be anything but searching, loaded with treasure and heartening. That's how I found this book to be and that's how I'm sure it will be for you too. I thank God for David and this 'conversation' he has given us on the task that is key to the future of the church.

SIMON MANCHESTER
Senior Mentor of the John Chapman Preaching Initiative,
Moore College, Sydney

PT RESOURCES

TEACHING
MARK

From text to message

ROBIN SYDSERFF

SERIES EDITORS: JON GEMMELL & DAVID JACKMAN

978-1-5271-0533-1

Teaching Mark

Robin Sydserff

Mark's gospel is a book that we think we know. It appears straight forward, fast paced and simple. However anyone who has spent any time engrossed in its pages will be aware that under the surface there is great depth and profundity. Robin has written *Teaching Mark* to help the preacher and teacher in the study to not just skim the surface of this life changing account but to go deep and see what is really there.

Robin Sydserff has preached through Mark three times in the last 10 years and taught this material in a variety of other contexts – it shows! He not only has a deep knowledge and love of the text but an infectious passion for the Lord Jesus Christ Himself. Mark's gospel is familiar to many but Teaching Mark *will help any bible study leader or preacher to hear God's voice more clearly and to teach His word more faithfully. It will inspire many to preach Christ and Him crucified from this great gospel!*

Paul Clarke
Senior Minister, St Andrews Free Church, Scotland

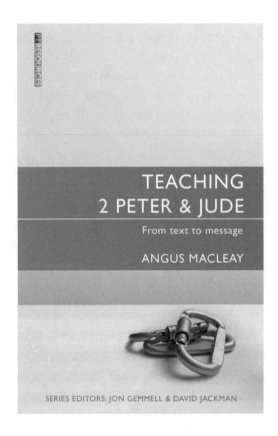

TEACHING
2 PETER & JUDE

From text to message

ANGUS MACLEAY

SERIES EDITORS: JON GEMMELL & DAVID JACKMAN

978-1-5271-0563-8

Teaching 2 Peter & Jude

Angus MacLeay

The books of 2 Peter and Jude are some of the least preached in the New Testament. However, these dynamic little books have an important message to be declared to the church in the 21st century. The need to 'contend for the faith' is vital in a confusing church landscape of compromise, pragmatism and drift. These books are dense and brimming with truth and so our hope is that this book helps you see all that is contained within their pages.

Teaching 2 Peter and Jude is a great addition to the growing 'Teaching the Bible' series. It will be a great aid to those who have the privilege and joy of teaching or preaching these particular books. Whether you are a small group leader, preacher, youth worker or someone who simply want help with their personal Bible study, this book will help you to comprehend and communicate the messages of 2 Peter and Jude.

The study embodies exactly the qualities it seeks to enable: humble listening to God's Word, wrestling with the literary structure, big idea, aim, illustration and application, a willingness to contend for the faith, a contending that is biblical in shape, tone and purpose, a fresh focus on the Lord Jesus Christ, a sustained determination to grow in knowledge of Christ, seasoned with wholesome realism about the ever present danger from false teaching. Every preacher will appreciate such prayerful wisdom, and the fruit from decades of preaching that lie behind a book of this quality.

Johnny Juckes
President, Oak Hill College, London

TEACHING
1 SAMUEL

From text to message

ANDREW REID

SERIES EDITORS: JON GEMMELL & DAVID JACKMAN

978-1-5271-0532-4

Teaching 1 Samuel

Andrew Reid

The book of 1 Samuel is a blockbuster. One of the most well-known books of the Old Testaments, its gripping narrative is dominated by big characters. Andrew Reid helps preachers get a handle on the vital part it plays in the unfolding story of the Bible.

It is so good to have the fruit of Andrew Reid's study of 1 Samuel now applied to how to be preaching this Old Testament book. Here we have an experienced guide helping us study God's Word carefully: there are no pre-packaged sermons (or Bible studies), but instead you will find yourself motivated to look again at the biblical text more carefully. I think the book is worth reading even for the 'Listening to the Whole of Scripture' sections in each chapter alone.

Neil Watkinson
International Director, Proclamation Trust

Christian Focus Publications

Our mission statement —

STAYING FAITHFUL
In dependence upon God we seek to impact the world through literature faithful to His infallible Word, the Bible. Our aim is to ensure that the Lord Jesus Christ is presented as the only hope to obtain forgiveness of sin, live a useful life and look forward to heaven with Him.

Our books are published in four imprints:

CHRISTIAN FOCUS

Popular works including biographies, commentaries, basic doctrine and Christian living.

CHRISTIAN HERITAGE

Books representing some of the best material from the rich heritage of the church.

MENTOR

Books written at a level suitable for Bible College and seminary students, pastors, and other serious readers. The imprint includes commentaries, doctrinal studies, examination of current issues and church history.

CF4•K

Children's books for quality Bible teaching and for all age groups: Sunday school curriculum, puzzle and activity books; personal and family devotional titles, biographies and inspirational stories – because you are never too young to know Jesus!

Christian Focus Publications Ltd,
Geanies House, Fearn, Ross-shire,
IV20 1TW, Scotland, United Kingdom.
www.christianfocus.com
blog.christianfocus.com